# The Catholic Connections Handbook

*For Middle Schoolers*

*Second Edition*

## CATECHIST GUIDE:
## THE OLD TESTAMENT, THE TRINITY, AND THE MISSION OF CHRIST

Virginia Halbur

Pray It! Study It! Live It!® resources offer a holistic approach to learning, living, and passing on the Catholic faith.

saint mary's press

The publishing team included Joanna Dailey, editor. Prepress and manufacturing coordinated by the production departments of Saint Mary's Press. We are also indebted to the authors of the first edition of the Saint Mary's Press® Catholic Connections Catechist Guides for their work, which has been incorporated into this revision: John Barone (Catholic Connections Catechist Guide, *Jesus the Christ*, © 2009), Chris Wardwell (Catholic Connections Catechist Guide, *God, Revelation, and Faith*, © 2009), and Gloria Shahin (Catholic Connections for Middle Schoolers, *Student Activity Booklet*, © 2010).

Cover image: © HixnHix / www.shutterstock.com

The scriptural quotations in this publication are from the Good News Translation® (Today's English Version, Second Edition). Copyright © 1992 by the American Bible Society. All rights reserved. Bible text from the Good News Translation is not to be reproduced in copies or otherwise by any means except as permitted in writing by the American Bible Society, 1865 Broadway, New York, NY 10023 (*www.americanbible.org*).

The quotation on page 8 is from *Meditations by John Baptist de La Salle*, translated by Richard Arnandez and Augustine Loes, edited by Augustine Loes and Francis Huether (Landover, MD: Christian Brothers Conference, 1994), page 440. Copyright © 1994 by Christian Brothers Conference. All rights reserved.

During this book's preparation, all citations, facts, figures, names, addresses, telephone numbers, Internet URLs, and other pieces of information cited within were verified for accuracy. The authors and Saint Mary's Press staff have made every attempt to reference current and valid sources, but we cannot guarantee the content of any source, and we are not responsible for any changes that may have occurred since our verification. If you find an error in, or have a question or concern about, any of the information or sources listed within, please contact Saint Mary's Press.

Printed in the United States of America

2258

ISBN 978-1-59982-360-7

# Contents

# Introduction

## Quick Overview

This guide is the parish catechist's resource for *The Catholic Connections Handbook for Middle Schoolers, Second Edition (CCH)*. The *CCH* is a comprehensive overview of the Catholic faith, in conformity with the *Catechism of the Catholic Church*. Its fifty chapters follow the outline of the Catholic faith as presented in the *Catechism* under the "four pillars" of faith: the Profession of Faith (the Creed), the Celebration of the Christian Mystery (the Sacraments), Life in Christ (Morality), and Christian Prayer. Thus, included in the *CCH* are the topics the Creed, liturgy and Sacraments, Christian morality, and prayer. Ten additional life issues chapters are found only in the catechist guides. The main text of each chapter in the *CCH* presents a particular topic of the Catholic faith. The sidebar articles in each chapter enhance the main text by connecting the topic to prayer, Catholic saints, Catholic history, and lived faith.

For the convenience of catechists, three separate guides accompany the *CCH*:

- *The Old Testament, the Trinity, and the Mission of Christ* (covering *CCH* chapters 1 through 18, and featuring two life issues chapters)

- *The New Testament, the Church, and the Sacraments* (covering *CCH* chapters 19 through 36, and featuring two life issues chapters)

- *Christian Morality and Prayer* (covering *CCH* chapters 37 through 50, and featuring six life issues chapters)

Each of these guides provides the teaching process for catechists to use in covering each chapter's content and connecting it to young people's life experience.

In preparation for creating these guides, we spent many hours observing and interviewing catechists and parish catechetical leaders. The lessons in this guide were created to directly respond to the needs we observed and the needs those leaders shared with us.

## Leading the Lessons

Each chapter in this guide is presented as a 60- to 90-minute lesson and provides time for the participants to read from the *CCH*. Each lesson is presented in a two-page spread so that you can teach the entire lesson without flipping back and forth between pages. Lessons follow the Saint Mary's Press Pray It! Study It! Live It! catechetical process that catechists have used with great success. Your preparation consists of familiarizing yourself with the *CCH* chapter content, reviewing the lesson in this guide, and gathering a few supplies.

Each lesson has four components: (1) a Pray It! segment found in the guide only and led by the catechist, or found in the Pray It! article in the *CCH*; (2) a Study It! segment; (3) a Live It! segment; and (4) a Pray It! segment found in the *CCH*. Each component is assigned a suggested time or time range. If your class is 60 minutes long, you will need to follow the shorter times; if your class is 75 or 90 minutes long, you can follow the longer times. Here is a quick look at the lesson components.

## Pray It! Opening Prayer

Each lesson begins with a short opening prayer related to the chapter topic. This prayer is found only in the guide, or sometimes in the Pray It! article in the *CCH*, to be led by the catechist. Suggestions are included for actively involving participant volunteers in the prayer.

## Study It!

The Study It! component is the heart of the lesson and will take the majority of your class time. During this time you will cover or review the chapter content. The Study It! process follows the chapter headings and is typically divided into three sections. Each section has a suggestion for beginning with a simple activity or discussion to prepare the young people for the content in the section. This is followed by reading or presenting that section's content in the *CCH*. A suggestion for reviewing the section content through questions and discussion is also provided.

You may read or present the content of the sections in a variety of ways. Here are some suggestions:

- Have the participants take turns reading the *CCH* section aloud, switching at each paragraph.

- Have the young people read the section silently to themselves.

- Ask the participants to read the chapter at home, prior to class. Review the content in class using the chapter summary handout.

- Present the content of each section in your own words, asking volunteers to read key sentences or paragraphs at appropriate times.

There is a lot of content in each chapter. It will not be possible to cover it all in depth, especially if your class is 60 minutes or less, so you will need to summarize some sections of the chapter quickly. The lesson directions suggest which sections to summarize, and the bullet points on the chapter summary handout provide key points to use.

## Live It!

The Live It! component is an engaging learning activity that connects the chapter content to the young people's life experience. These activities are typically about 15 minutes long, requiring a minimum of supplies and usually having the participants work together. If your class time is short, you will need to stay on top of the time and keep moving the process forward without too much delay. If your class time is longer, you can allow more time for the participants to interact with the content and with one another.

## Pray It! Closing Prayer

The lesson concludes with another simple prayer, using the prayer from the Pray It! article in the *CCH*. Suggestions are included for actively involving participant volunteers in the prayer.

# Handouts

The lesson for each chapter of the *CCH* has two one-page handouts designed to make your life as a catechist a little easier. The first handout is the chapter summary handout. On it are two or three learning objectives that are the main goals of the lesson. The chapter summary handout also contains a summary of the key content in the chapter. This handout can be used in the following ways:

- to help you prepare for leading the lesson with a quick overview of the main content points

- to hand out to the young people as a review of the chapter content

- to send home to parents and guardians so they are aware of, and can reinforce, what their son or daughter is learning in the lessons

The second handout is typically used as a learning resource for the Study It! or Live It! components of the lesson process. Sometimes it will contain a prayer to use during the Pray It! component. This activity handout is often integral to the presentation of the lesson, but sometimes it is offered as an optional activity that can be used to extend and enhance the lesson. This optional activity handout can be used as a take-home activity. The variety of activity handouts allows for some to be used as discussion starters; some as informal, quick checks of the content presented; some as an aid to individual or group work; and some as a means to encourage creativity and personal expression in learning.

## Online Content

All of the handouts in this guide are also available online for easy access and customization. Also available online are a variety of other resources that can be used to reinforce the content covered in a lesson and provide additional support for lesson planning. These resources include:

- chapter quizzes

- tip sheets for catechists and parents

- links to helpful websites

- additional activity handouts

Go to *www.smp.org/resourcecenter/books/* to see how these support materials might help you.

## Spirit and Life

As a catechist, you have taken on an exciting and profoundly important task. Saint John Baptist de La Salle, the patron saint of teachers, often reminded his teachers that their students were not simply students in an academic sense but were *disciples*: "This must be your goal when you instruct your disciples, that they live a Christian life and that your words become spirit and life for them" (Loes and Huether, eds., Meditations by John Baptist de La Salle, p. 440). As a Lasallian ministry, Saint Mary's Press has this goal as well—that as you use and adapt these guides in your own situation, your words may become spirit and life for your own disciples. We at Saint Mary's Press are deeply appreciative of your ministry and hope that our resources serve you well. Please be assured of our continual prayers for you and the young people you serve.

# Part 1: The Creed

# Chapter 1

## Revelation, Sacred Scripture, and Sacred Tradition

### Preparation and Supplies

- Study chapter 1, "Revelation, Sacred Scripture, and Sacred Tradition," in the handbook.
- Provide a Bible for each participant, if possible.
- Make copies of the chapter 1 activity handout, "Scripture Passage Search" (Document #: TX003497), one for each group of three or four.

### Pray It! (5 minutes)

**Lead** the participants in making the Sign of the Cross. Pray the following:

> ➤ God, we thank you for bringing us here today. May this time we spend together bring us closer to one another and closer to you. We ask that you make yourself known to us. We cannot see you or hear you or touch you, but we know you are here. Please speak to our hearts. Make us aware of your presence. Amen.

**Invite** the participants to offer any special intentions for which they would like to pray. **Close** with the Sign of the Cross.

### Study It! (40 to 50 minutes, depending on your class length)

#### A. Revelation

1. Briefly **explain** that the topic for this chapter is God's Revelation. Ask if anyone knows what the word *revelation* means. **Ask** if anyone knows a word that sounds similar (reveal). **Explain** that this is essentially what Revelation is: God's revealing himself, or making himself known, to us.
2. **Direct** the participants to read the chapter introduction and the section "Revelation," on pages 16–19 in the handbook. The content covers points 1 through 4 on the handout "Chapter 1 Summary" (Document #: TX003496).
3. *(Optional)* **Direct** the participants to the Think About It! article on page 19. **Ask** a volunteer to read the article aloud, and **use** the questions at the end to lead a discussion.

#### B. Sacred Scripture

1. **Distribute** a Bible to each participant. Increase the participants' familiarity with the Bible by reviewing the sections of the Bible. **Instruct** the young people to locate and hold the pages of the sections. **Demonstrate** how they should do this. **Ask** them to hold the Old Testament in the fingers of their left hand and the New Testament in the fingers of their right hand. **Invite** volunteers to share their observations. **Point out** that the Old Testament is more than twice the size of the New Testament.

**Ask** the participants to hold the pages of the Gospels. **Point out** that there are four Gospels—Matthew, Mark, Luke, and John. **Invite** the young people to share any observations they may have. (For example, Mark's Gospel is the shortest, and Luke's is the longest.)

**Ask** the participants to hold the pages of the Acts of the Apostles through the end of the Bible. **Explain** that the rest of the Bible covers the struggles, works, and teachings of the early Christian Church. **Ask** the young people if they have any questions.

2. **Direct** the participants to read the sections "Sacred Scripture" and "Sacred Tradition" on pages 19–22. The content covers points 5 through 8 on the handout "Chapter 1 Summary" (Document #: TX003496).

3. *(Optional)* **Direct** the young people to the Live It! article on page 21 in the handbook. **Invite** a volunteer to read the article aloud, and **use** the questions at the end to lead a discussion.

## C. God's Mystery

**Direct** the participants to read the section "God's Mystery," on page 23 in the handbook. The content covers point 9 on the handout "Chapter 1 Summary" (Document #: TX003496). *Note:* If you are running short on time, you may wish to just briefly summarize this section.

# Live It! (10 to 15 minutes)

1. **Organize** the young people into groups of three or four, and **distribute** the chapter 1 activity handout, "Scripture Passage Search" (Document #: TX003497), to each group. **Divide** and **assign** the Scripture passages listed in the handout among the groups. **Explain** the task as follows:
   ➢ Members of each group are to look up their Scripture passages and take turns reading them aloud to one another. *(You may wish to practice locating one or more Scripture passages with the large group before the groups work independently.)*
2. **Invite** volunteers from each small group to share their favorite passages with the large group.
3. **Comment** as follows in your own words:
   ➢ What God has made known about himself is called Revelation. It is communicated to the world in two main ways: through Sacred Scripture and through Sacred Tradition.
   ➢ God fully revealed himself in Jesus Christ.
   ➢ The responsibility of teaching about Jesus Christ, through Scripture and Tradition, belongs to the Apostles and their successors, the Pope and the bishops.
   ➢ The seventy-three inspired books and letters we recognize as the Word of God comprise Sacred Scripture. The Bible is another name for Sacred Scripture.
   ➢ God is the ultimate author of the Bible, for the Holy Spirit inspired the human authors to communicate, without error, what God wants us to know for our salvation. This guidance of the Holy Spirit is called inspiration.

# Closing Prayer (5 minutes)

**Gather** the participants in a circle. **Ask** them to take out their handbooks and turn to the Pray It! article on page 17. When all are ready, **ask** a volunteer to read the prayer aloud. **Invite** another volunteer to read Romans 8:38–39 aloud. **Close** with the Sign of the Cross.

# Online Resources

To access activities and a quiz related to this chapter, go to *www.smp.org/resourcecenter/books/* and click on "Catechist: Additional Course Handouts or Quizzes." Tip sheets and links are also available.

# Revelation, Sacred Scripture, and Sacred Tradition

## Chapter 1 Summary

### Chapter Learning Objectives

- The participants will explore how God reveals himself to us, particularly through Sacred Scripture and Sacred Tradition.

- The participants will become familiar with the sections of the Bible.

### Content Summary

1. God makes himself known to us through the signs of creation around us, through the voice of the Church, and through the voices of our conscience speaking from within us.

2. What God has made known about himself is called *Revelation*. It is communicated to the world in two main ways: through Sacred Scripture and through Sacred Tradition.

3. God fully revealed himself in Jesus Christ.

4. The responsibility of teaching about Jesus Christ, through Scripture and Tradition, belongs to the Apostles and their successors, the Pope and the bishops.

5. The seventy-three inspired books and letters we recognize as the Word of God comprise Sacred Scripture. The Bible is another name for Sacred Scripture.

6. God is the ultimate author of the Bible, for the Holy Spirit inspired the human authors to communicate, without error, what God wants us to know for our salvation. This guidance of the Holy Spirit is called inspiration.

7. Four special books in the New Testament are called the Gospels. The Gospels tell us about the life, teachings, death, and Resurrection of Jesus Christ.

8. The word *tradition* means "to hand on." *Sacred Tradition* means both the central content of the Catholic faith and the way that content has been handed down through the centuries under the guidance of the Holy Spirit.

9. We cannot totally grasp God, because God is greater than anything we can understand. God is the ultimate mystery.

# Chapter 1 Activity: Scripture Passage Search

Look up some or all of the following Scripture passages:

- Matthew 6:9–15 (The Our Father)

- Exodus 2:1–10 (Moses and the Burning Bush)

- Isaiah 7:10–16 (Prophecy of the Birth of Emmanuel)

- Jeremiah 1:4–10 (Call of the Young Prophet Jeremiah)

- Zechariah 9:9–10 (Prophecy of the Lord Entering Jerusalem)

- Psalm 23 (The Lord Is My Shepherd)

- 1 Corinthians 13:1–13 (Saint Paul's Discourse on Love)

- Matthew 7:12 (The Golden Rule)

- Matthew 5:3–10 (The Beatitudes)

- Matthew 18:10–14 (The Parable of the Lost Sheep)

- Matthew 22:34–40 (The Greatest Commandment)

- Mark 4:35–41 (The Calming of the Storm at Sea)

- Mark 10:13–16 (The Blessing of the Children)

- Mark 12:28–34 (The Greatest Commandment)

- Mark 14:22–26 (The Last Supper)

- Luke 6:37–42 (On Not Judging Others)

- Luke 15:11–32 (The Parable of the Lost [Prodigal] Son)

- Luke 21:1–4 (The Poor Widow's Donation)

- Luke 23:39–46 (The Agony in the Garden)

- John 1:1–5 (The Word and the Light)

- John 8:12 (The Light of the World)

- John 15:1–17 (The Vine and the Branches, Last Supper Discourse)

- John 20:1–10 (The Resurrection)

- 2 Timothy 3:10–17 (Saint Paul's Reminder to Timothy about Learning from Scripture)

Document #: TX003497

# Chapter 2

# The Bible: God's Plan for Salvation

## Preparation and Supplies

- Study chapter 2, "The Bible: God's Plan for Salvation," in the handbook.
- Clear a reasonably sized area of the room to enable the participants to walk freely without bumping into anything.
- Gather sheets of colored construction paper and a blindfold.
- Make copies of the chapter 2 activity handout, "A Salvation History Timeline" (Document #: TX003499), one for each group of two or three.
- Provide Bibles, one for each group.

## Pray It! (5 minutes)

**Tell** the participants that this class will begin with a prayer asking for God's guidance on life's journey. **Pray** the following:

> ➤ Father, throughout history you have guided us. Though sometimes it is difficult to hear you, we still listen. Though sometimes we make the wrong choices, you give us a second chance and call us back home to you. You made all of us good. You made all of us to be with you. Please be patient with us. We love you and are thankful for all you have given us. We lift up this prayer in the name of the Father, and of the Son, and of the Holy Spirit. Amen.

## Study It! (40 to 50 minutes, depending on your class length)

### A. The Early Stages of Salvation History (Stages 1, 2, and 3)

1.  **Direct** the young people to find a partner. If there is an odd number of participants, have one group of three. **Inform** the young people that this game is called Mine Field. **Explain** the following:

    > ➤ One pair at a time will leave the room and blindfold one of its members. While the pair is gone, I will place a number of colored sheets of paper on the floor, creating a "mine field." When the pair returns, the non-blindfolded person will have the task of guiding his or her blindfolded partner through the mine field without stepping on any of the papers. The non-blindfolded person will do this only by offering spoken directions as a guide.

    **Reassure** the participants that they will be safe. After you have chosen the first pair, **give** them the blindfold and **ask** them to leave the room. While they are gone, **arrange** the sheets of construction paper on the floor. Be sure you have covered the floor well, leaving little open space to walk. **Ask** the first pair to enter the room and begin their walk through the mind field. **Repeat** the activity until all the groups have had a turn. **Reflect** on the experience afterward by discussing how the young people felt walking through the mind field, what they did to get through it successfully, and what made the experience difficult.

2.  **Direct** the participants to read the chapter introduction and the sections "Stage 1: Primeval History," "Stage 2: The Patriarchs," and "Stage 3: Egypt and the Exodus," on pages 24–28 in the handbook. The content covers points 1 through 3 on the handout "Chapter 2 Summary" (Document #: TX003498).

3. *(Optional)* **Direct** the participants to the Think About It! article on page 29 in the hand-book. **Ask** a volunteer to read the article aloud, and **use** the questions at the end to lead a discussion.

## B. The Middle Stages of Salvation History (Stages 4, 5, and 6)

1. **Explain** to the young people that God has a plan of salvation in which everyone has a part. **Ask** the participants to name people they know personally who are doing what God intended, and ask them to explain their choices.

2. **Direct** the young people to read the sections "Stage 4: The Promised Land and the Judges," "Stage 5: The Kings and the Prophets," and "Stage 6: The Exile and the Return," on pages 29–32 in the handbook. The content covers point 3 on the handout "Chapter 2 Summary" (Document #: TX003498).

3. *(Optional)* **Direct** the participants to the Live It! article on page 31 in the handbook. **Read** the article aloud, and **brainstorm** with the young people ways they can participate in God's plan of salvation.

## C. The Last Stages of Salvation History (Stages 7 and 8)

**Direct** the participants to read the sections "Stage 7: The Life of Jesus Christ" and "Stage 8: The Church," on pages 33–34 in the handbook. The content covers points 4 through 7 on the hand-out "Chapter 2 Summary" (Document #: TX003498).

*Note:* If you are running short on time, you may wish to just briefly summarize this section.

## Live It! (15 to 20 minutes)

1. **Organize** the young people into groups of two or three. **Distribute** a Bible and a copy of the handout "A Salvation History Timeline" (Document #: TX003499) to each group. **Explain** the task as follows:

   ➤ Each group is to put the events listed on the handout in chronological order by numbering them 1 through 10. You may use your Bibles to locate the events. In the empty squares on the handout, draw three symbols to represent events from salvation history.

2. **Invite** volunteers to read the events aloud chronologically. **Ask** a representative from each group to share the symbols the group drew in the squares and to explain what events they represent.

3. **Comment** as follows in your own words:

   ➤ The final stage of salvation history continues today through the Church.
   ➤ The Church will continue to share the Gospel until the end of time.
   ➤ With the help of the Holy Spirit, we, as members of the Church, take part in Christ's mission today.

## Closing Prayer (5 minutes)

**Direct** the participants to the Pray It! article on page 25 in the handbook. **Lead** them in praying the prayer together. **Close** with the Sign of the Cross.

## Online Resources

To access activities and a quiz related to this chapter, go to *www.smp.org/resourcecenter/books/* and click on "Catechist: Additional Course Handouts or Quizzes." Tip sheets and links are also available.

# The Bible: God's Plan for Salvation

## Chapter 2 Summary

### Chapter Learning Objectives

- The participants will explore ways God has guided humanity through a number of events in salvation history.

- The participants will examine the Bible to see examples of people chosen by God to do his will.

- The participants will reflect on how they participate in salvation history.

### Content Summary

1. Salvation history is the pattern of events through which God reveals himself and his saving actions to us.

2. Salvation history can be divided into eight stages—six stages found in the Old Testament, and two stages found in the New Testament.

3. The Old Testament stages are the following: (1) primeval history, (2) the patriarchs, (3) Egypt and the Exodus, (4) the Promised Land and the judges, (5) the kings and the prophets, and (6) the Exile and the return.

4. The New Testament stages are the following: (7) the life of Jesus Christ and (8) the Church.

5. The final stage of salvation history continues today through the Church.

6. The Church will continue to share the Gospel until the end of time.

7. We, as members of the Church and with the help of the Holy Spirit, take part in Christ's mission today.

(All summary points are taken from *The Catholic Connections Handbook for Middle Schoolers, Second Edition*. Copyright © 2014 by Saint Mary's Press. All rights reserved.)

# Chapter 2 Activity: A Salvation History Time Line

Put the following events in chronological order by numbering them 1 through 10. In the empty squares, draw three symbols to represent events from salvation history.

_____ Abraham and Sarah's descendants became God's people, the Israelites.

_____ Adam and Eve disobeyed God by eating from the forbidden tree.

_____ God made a covenant with Noah never to destroy the human race with a flood again.

_____ Through Moses, God gave the Ten Commandments to the Israelites to guide them in living their part of the covenant they made with God.

_____ Adam and Eve were driven out of the Garden of Eden.

_____ God established the New Covenant with all people by sending his only Son to become one of us.

_____ God wiped out all human wickedness from the earth with a flood.

_____ God made a covenant with Abraham and promised him many descendants.

_____ God created Adam and Eve and promised them they would live with him in happiness forever.

_____ Moses led the Israelites out of slavery in Egypt.

# Chapter 3

**3**

# God the Father

## Preparation and Supplies

- Study chapter 3, "God the Father," in the handbook.
- Draw an outline of a person on a sheet of newsprint. Write the following heading at the top of the newsprint: "The Best Qualities of Human Fathers." Place the newsprint in the middle of the meeting space where the participants can access it.
- Write the name of each participant on individual slips of paper and put them in a basket.
- Gather for each young person a cardboard packing box or carton (medium size, with sides about 10 inches high), wrapping paper, ribbon, gift tags, construction paper in various colors, glue, tape, scissors, markers.
- Make copies of the chapter 3 activity handout, "The Mystery of God" (Document #: TX003501), one for each participant.

## Pray It! (5 minutes)

**Tell** the participants that class will begin with a prayer to God the Father. **Lead** them in making the Sign of the Cross. **Pray** the following prayer:

> ➤ God our Father, we gather to ask for your guidance. Remind us that you are always near, ready to love and care for us as your children. Amen.

**Direct** the young people to silently pray to God as their Father, asking for his guidance in their lives. **Close** with the Sign of the Cross.

## Study It! (35 to 45 minutes, depending on your class length)

### A. Who Is God?

1. **Ask** the participants the following question:

   > ➤ What good qualities do human fathers have?

   As volunteers share their ideas, invite them to come forward and write the qualities on the outline of a person on the newsprint.

2. **Direct** the young people to read the chapter introduction and the section "Who Is God?" on pages 36–39 in the handbook. The content covers point 1 on the handout "Chapter 3 Summary" (Document #: TX003500).

3. *(Optional)* **Direct** the participants to the painting by Michelangelo on page 36 in the handbook. **Use** the questions in the caption to lead a discussion.

### B. The Trinity

1. **Invite** volunteers to share what God has done throughout history. **Ask** each volunteer to write on the board what the action says about God and who he is. For example, if a young person says that God created the world, she or he should write "Creator" on the board.

2. **Direct** the participants to read the sections "The Trinity" and "God the Father," on pages 39–42 in the handbook. The content covers points 2 through 6 on the handout "Chapter 3 Summary" (Document #: TX003500).

3. *(Optional)* **Direct** the young people to the Think About It! article on page 41 in the handbook. **Ask** a volunteer to read the article aloud, and **use** the questions at the end to lead a discussion.

## C. God Is Truth and Love

**Direct** participants to read the section "God Is Truth and Love," on pages 42–43 in the handbook. The content covers point 7 on the handout "Chapter 3 Summary" (Document #: TX003500).

*Note:* If you are running short on time, you may wish to just briefly summarize this section.

# Live It! (15 to 20 minutes)

1. **Distribute** a gift box to each young person and make the construction materials readily available to all. **Brainstorm** ideas about gifts God has given us, both small and large. **Tell** the participants to think of as many small and large gifts as they can. **Write** these on the board. (Gifts might include the sun, the moon, the stars, the world, our families, animals, flowers, the smile of a friend.)

2. **Ask** the young people to select a name from the basket. If anyone draws his or her own name, he or she should draw again. **Explain** the task as follows:
   ➤ The name on the slip of paper you drew from the basket is the person for whom you will be making a gift.
   ➤ Use the construction materials that I have provided to make a three-dimensional paper sculpture of a gift for this person. You can use one of the ideas listed on the board or come up with your own idea for a gift. The gift must be able to fit inside your gift box and should be one that the person might especially appreciate.
   ➤ Spread out as much as possible, and do not look at what others are making. When you have finished making the gift, place it in the box, wrap it, and write the person's name on the gift tag.

3. After everyone has had time to create and wrap his or her gift, **share** the following comments in your own words:
   ➤ God is our Father, and he has given us many gifts. The greatest gift that God gave us is his only Son, Jesus. He also sent the Holy Spirit to be with us always. There is no greater sign of love than this.

   *(Note:* The gift exchange will happen after the closing prayer.)

# Optional Activity

**Distribute** copies of the chapter 3 activity handout, "The Mystery of God" (Document #: TX003501), to the participants and **ask** them to complete the crossword puzzle.

# Closing Prayer (5 minutes)

**Direct** the participants to the Pray It! article on page 37 in the handbook. **Lead** them in praying the prayer together. **Close** by inviting the young people to exchange the gifts they created.

# Online Resources

To access activities and a quiz related to this chapter, go to *www.smp.org/resourcecenter/books/* and click on "Catechist: Additional Course Handouts or Quizzes." Tip sheets and links are also available.

# God the Father

## Chapter 3 Summary

### Chapter Learning Objectives

- The participants will examine how God has revealed himself to us, especially in the image of Father.

- The participants will reflect on ways to nurture their relationships with God, family, and friends.

### Content Summary

1. God revealed himself to Moses as I AM, or Yahweh. This name expresses the power and infinity of God.

2. God has revealed himself as the Father, the Son, and the Holy Spirit—one God in three Divine Persons who is the Holy Trinity.

3. Belief in God as Trinity is the central belief of all Christians.

4. Even when God reveals himself to us, he is essentially mystery. No human being can completely know or understand God.

5. God the Father is all-powerful, all-knowing, and everywhere. Although God is neither male nor female, we call God "Father," as Jesus did.

6. God is eternal and beyond time, the one who is, always was, and always will be.

7. God is Truth and Love. God created us out of love and always keeps his promises. God the Father gave us his only Son and sent the Holy Spirit to be with us always. There is no greater sign of love than this.

(All summary points are taken from *The Catholic Connections Handbook for Middle Schoolers, Second Edition*. Copyright © 2014 by Saint Mary's Press. All rights reserved.)

# Chapter 3 Activity: The Mystery of God

Complete the Scripture quotes and sentences to solve the crossword puzzle about the mystery of God.

**Across**

3. God always keeps his _____.

5. "My thoughts," says the LORD," are not like yours. . . . / As high as the _____ are above the earth, / so high are my ways and thoughts above yours" (Isaiah 55:8–9).

6. "No one knows the _____ except the Son and those to whom the Son chooses to reveal him" (Matthew 11:27).

7. "Whoever does not love does not know _____, for God is love" (1 John 4:8).

**Down**

1. We say that God is _____ simply because what he tells us is true.

2. Whatever we know about God, we know because he _____ it to us.

4. "I will comfort you . . . as a _____ comforts her child" (Isaiah 66:13).

6. God is always _____ to his people.

Document #: TX003501

# Chapter 4
# The Holy Trinity

## Preparation and Supplies

- Study chapter 4, "The Holy Trinity," in the handbook.
- Provide a sheet of poster board, glue, scissors, and a selection of magazines, enough for each group of four or five.
- Make copies of the chapter 4 activity handout, "Symbols for the Blessed Trinity" (Document #: TX003503), one for each participant.

## Pray It! (5 minutes)

**Tell** the young people that class will begin with a prayer to the Holy Trinity. **State** the following in your own words:

> ➢ God is Father, Son, and Holy Spirit. God is the unity of the three Persons as one God.
> ➢ To understand this concept, think of a time when a friend or family member was sad, and his or her sadness made you sad. Or perhaps you felt the joy when he or she accomplished something wonderful. You experienced unity or oneness with another person, yet remained your distinct self.
> ➢ Sometimes we experience oneness and unity when we give our time and effort to help someone in need.

Allow the participants a moment to reflect, and then **direct** them to the Pray It! article on page 45 in the handbook and lead them in saying the prayer together.

## Study It! (35 to 45 minutes, depending on your class length)

### A. One God, Three Persons

1. **Ask** the young people to reflect on times they turned to God with hope and trust when they faced a difficult situation. **Invite** volunteers to share their experiences and tell how their faith in God helped them face the difficulty. **Direct** the participants' attention to the picture on page 44. **Ask** a volunteer to interpret this image as reflecting our relationship with the Father, Son, and Holy Spirit.

2. **Direct** the participants to read the chapter introduction and the section "One God, Three Divine Persons," on pages 44–47 in the handbook. The content covers points 1 through 4 on the handout "Chapter 4 Summary" (Document #: TX003502).

3. **Direct** the young people to the Think About It! article on page 47. **Invite** a volunteer to read the article aloud, and **use** the questions at the end to lead a discussion.

### B. The Work of the Trinity

1. **Draw** a circle on the board and divide it into three equal parts. **Label** one section "the Father," another "the Son," and the third "the Holy Spirit." **Ask** the participants whether this is an accurate depiction of the Trinity. **Invite** a volunteer to explain why it is inaccurate.

**Explain** the following in your own words:

> ➢ God cannot be split into parts. Whenever the Father does something, the Son and the Holy Spirit are acting too. Whenever the Son acts, the Father and the Holy Spirit are at work.

2. **Direct** the young people to read the section "The Work of the Trinity," on pages 47–49 in the handbook. The content covers points 5 through 9 on the handout "Chapter 4 Summary" (Document #: TX003502).

3. *(Optional)* **Distribute** and **use** the chapter 4 activity handout, "Symbols for the Blessed Trinity" (Document #: TX003503), to reinforce the participants' understanding of the concept of the Holy Trinity.

## C. The Trinity Is a Communion

**Direct** the participants to read the section "The Trinity Is a Communion," on pages 49–50 in the handbook. The content covers point 10 on the handout "Chapter 4 Summary" (Document #: TX003502).

*Note:* If you are running short on time, you may wish to just briefly summarize this section.

# Live It! (15 to 20 minutes)

1. **Organize** the large group into groups of four or five. Give each group a sheet of poster board, glue, scissors, and a selection of magazines. **Explain** the task as follows:

> ➢ Each group is to cut out pictures from the magazines that reflect the community of the Father, Son, and Holy Spirit and glue them onto the poster board to create a collage.
>
> ➢ The pictures should reflect unity, harmony, and love. The collage can include pictures of mothers, fathers, boys, and girls. You can also use symbols like buildings, clouds, or animals—anything that fits the theme of unity, harmony, and love.

> (*Note:* As the groups are working, pay close attention to their conversations. Make mental notes of how the groups reflect the unity, harmony, and love you just discussed.)

2. After 10 minutes **invite** each group to briefly present its collage to the large group. When all the groups have presented, **invite** volunteers to share examples of how they reflected the unity, harmony, and love of the Trinity while they worked on their collages. **Add** your own observations after the volunteers share.

3. **Comment** as follows in your own words:

> ➢ It is important to talk about the Trinity, but it is far more important to do what the Trinity does: to live in unity, harmony, and love with one another.

# Closing Prayer (5 minutes)

**Direct** the participants to turn to pages 554 in the handbook and pray the Act of Faith together. **Close** with the Sign of the Cross.

# Online Resources

To access activities and a quiz related to this chapter, go to *www.smp.org/resourcecenter/books/* and click on "Catechist: Additional Course Handouts or Quizzes." Tip sheets and links are also available.

# The Holy Trinity

## Chapter 4 Summary

### Chapter Learning Objectives

- The participants will identify the Trinity as three Divine Persons in one God—Father, Son, and Holy Spirit.

- The participants will explore ways that humans can reflect the unity, harmony, and love that exist in the Trinity.

### Content Summary

1. The one God has revealed himself as the Father, the Son, and the Holy Spirit—one God in three Divine Persons who is the Holy Trinity.

2. The central mystery of our Christian life and faith is the Trinity.

3. Each Person of the Trinity does not make up one-third of the whole God. The complete presence of God can be found in each of them. The Father, the Son, and the Holy Spirit cannot be separated from one another.

4. The three distinct Persons are wholly united, not just by their actions but by who they are: one Divine Being.

5. All the works of God are done by all three Persons.

6. Yet some of God's works are more strongly associated with the Father, the Son, or the Holy Spirit.

7. God the Father is the First Person of the Blessed Trinity. God the Father is the source from which life comes. Although God the Son and God the Holy Spirit also created the world, it is natural to think of God the Father when we think of the Creator.

8. God the Son is the Second Person of the Blessed Trinity. When he became man, he was given the name Jesus. Later, he was also given the title Christ, or Anointed One. We call Jesus Christ the Savior to recognize his saving actions, but the Father and the Holy Spirit also save us.

9. God the Holy Spirit is the Third Divine Person of the Blessed Trinity, who inspires us, guides us, and makes us holy. Although the Gifts of the Holy Spirit are also given by the Father and the Son, it is proper to recognize them as being from the Holy Spirit.

10. The Trinity is a communion of the three Divine Persons: the Father, the Son, and the Holy Spirit. The Trinity is a perfect community of harmony and love. We share in this love and harmony of the Trinity through family life and through service to our local community and our world.

Document #: TX003502

# Chapter 4 Activity:
# Symbols for the Blessed Trinity

According to tradition, Saint Patrick used a shamrock to represent the Blessed Trinity—the one God in three Divine Persons. The following symbols, the triquetra (TRY-kwetra), on the left, and the triangle, are also symbols for the Trinity. On the lines below, explain how each of these symbols is a good representation for the Trinity.

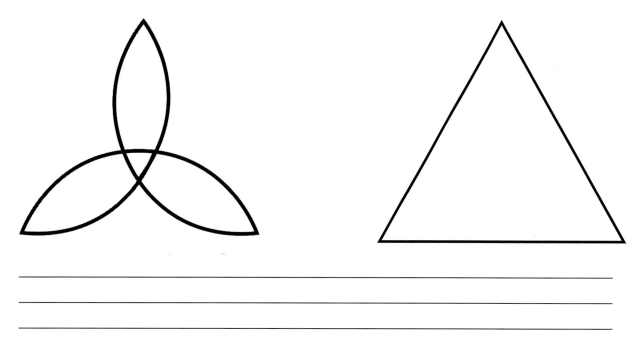

_____

_____

_____

_____

_____

## A Prayer to the Trinity

Solve the following cryptogram to decipher a simple prayer in which we recognize the mystery of one God in three Divine Persons.

| A | B | C | D | E | F | G | H | I | J | K | L | M | N | O | P | Q | R | S | T | U | V | W | X | Y | Z |
|---|---|---|---|---|---|---|---|---|---|---|---|---|---|---|---|---|---|---|---|---|---|---|---|---|---|
| 1 |   |   |   |   |   |   |   | 14 |   |   |   |   |   |   |   |   |   | 24 |   |   |   |   |   |   |   |

I __  __ __ __     A __ __ __     __ __     __ __ __     A __ __ __ __ __ ,
14 18   22 13 26    18 1 8 26      19 21    22 13 26      21 1 22 13 26 5

A __ __  __ __  __ __ __   S __ __ ,  A __ __   __ __  __ __ __
1 18 10  19 21  22 13 26   24 19 18   1 18 10   19 21  22 13 26

__ __ __ __   S __ I __ I __ .

# Chapter 5

# The Bible: The Old Testament

**5**

## Preparation and Supplies

- Study chapter 5, "The Bible: The Old Testament," in the handbook.
- Provide sheets of blank 8½-x-11-inch paper, one for each participant.
- Provide a Bible for each group of two or three.
- Make copies of the chapter 5 activity handout, "Finding God's Guidance in the Bible" (Document #: TX003505), one for each group of two or three.

## Pray It! (5 minutes)

**Tell** the participants that class will begin with a prayer to help us reflect on how God has been present and actively working to help us be united with him. **Pray** the following:

> ➤ God the Father, throughout history you have acted to bring about our salvation. You established a covenant with Abraham; you gave us the Commandments through Moses; you sent the prophets to guide us; you sent your Son, Jesus Christ, to save us; and you sent the Apostles out to continue spreading the Good News.
>
> Yet, what we read in the Bible is not the end of the story. You continue to guide us today, even in ways we do not notice.
>
> Father, encourage us to be open to you. Give us the strength to acknowledge your work even in painful moments. Give us the faith to trust you and to follow your will.
>
> We ask this in Jesus' name. Amen.

## Study It! (40 to 50 minutes, depending on your class length)

### A. The Pentateuch

1. **Ask** the young people to name some of the countries their ancestors came from. **Record** their answers on the board. **Ask** the participants to list some of the customs and traditions that each of the countries listed are known for. **Invite** the young people to brainstorm ways they can learn about their family's heritage. Be sure to mention the following if the participants fail to mention them: oral history handed on from generation to generation; letters, genealogies, written history, poetry and other forms of literature; art and photographs.

2. **Direct** the young people to read the chapter introduction and the section "The Pentateuch," on pages 52–56 in the handbook. The content covers points 1 through 4 on the handout "Chapter 5 Summary" (Document #: TX003504).

3. *(Optional)* **Direct** the participants to the Live It! article on page 58. **Ask** a volunteer to read the article aloud. **Distribute** to each young person a sheet of 8½-x-11-inch paper, and **instruct** them to draw a horizontal line across the middle with the paper set lengthwise. At the far left side of the line, **ask** them to write the date they were born. At the far right side of the line, **ask** them to write today's date. **Tell** them to think back to events and people in their childhood that brought them closer to God. **Instruct** them to fill in their time lines by inserting the names of those people and events.

## B. The Historical Books and the Wisdom and Poetry Books

1. **Explain** to the participants that we are all imperfect and have flaws. Some people can do things that others cannot. **Brainstorm** with the young people ways that imperfections and flaws can bring us closer to one another and how they can bring us closer to God. **Record** their answers on the board.

2. **Direct** the participants to read the sections "The Historical Books" and "The Wisdom and Poetry Books," on pages 56–64 in the handbook. The content covers points 5 and 6 on the handout "Chapter 5 Summary" (Document #: TX003504).

3. *(Optional)* **Direct** the young people to the Think About It! article on page 59. **Invite** a volunteer to read the article aloud, and **use** the questions at the end to lead a discussion.

## C. The Prophets

**Direct** the participants to read the section "The Prophets," on pages 65–67 in the handbook. The content covers points 7 and 8 on the handout "Chapter 5 Summary" (Document #: TX003504). *Note:* If you are running short on time, you may wish to just briefly summarize this section.

## Live It! (10 to 15 minutes)

1. **Organize** the young people into groups of two or three. **Distribute** a Bible and a copy of the chapter 5 activity, "Finding God's Guidance in the Bible" (Document #: TX003505), to each group. **Assign** one or two of the readings to each group. **Explain** the task as follows:
   - ➢ Each group is to locate and read the Scripture passages it has been assigned.
   - ➢ After reading each passage, your group is to discuss and answer the questions at the top of the handout.

2. **Invite** volunteers from each group to share the results of their discussions.

3. **Comment** as follows in your own words:
   - ➢ Understanding the Chosen People's relationship with God helps us to grow in our understanding of our faith. We do this by studying and praying with the Old Testament.

## Closing Prayer (5 minutes)

**Direct** the participants to the Pray It! article on page 53 in the handbook. **Organize** the large group into two groups. **Instruct** the two groups to take turns reading the lines of the psalm aloud. **Close** with the Sign of the Cross.

## Online Resources

To access activities and a quiz related to this chapter, go to *www.smp.org/resourcecenter/books/* and click on "Catechist: Additional Course Handouts or Quizzes." Tip sheets and links are also available.

# The Bible: The Old Testament

## Chapter 5 Summary

### Chapter Learning Objectives

- The participants will examine the four sections of the Old Testament and some important people and events found in them.

- The participants will explore how understanding the Chosen People's relationship with God helps us to understand our own faith better.

### Content Summary

1. Jesus was a Jew. Our faith is built upon the Jewish faith practiced by Jesus. We are the spiritual descendants of the Jewish people.

2. To understand our faith better, it helps to understand the Chosen People's relationship with God. We do this by studying and praying with the Old Testament.

3. The Old Testament is divided into four major sections: the Pentateuch, the historical books, the wisdom and poetry books, and the prophets.

4. The Pentateuch is the first five books of the Bible: Genesis, Exodus, Leviticus, Numbers, and Deuteronomy. These books teach us about God's plan for salvation.

5. The historical books were written to emphasize God's actions in history.

6. The wisdom and poetry books include teachings on ways to be a wise person, to live a good and holy life. The poetry books include songs of praise, wise sayings, advice on living a good life, and a song celebrating love between a man and a woman, symbolizing God and his people.

7. The books of the prophets reveal the preaching of various prophets, usually touching on the failures of God's people: idolatry, injustice, and false worship. The messages of the prophets also include messages of hope: God is faithful, the faithful will survive, God will send a Messiah.

8. The Holy Spirit continues to act in the Church today, bringing people to Christ. The Holy Spirit helps us to understand Jesus' death and Resurrection, and makes the mystery of Christ present in the Eucharist and in the other Sacraments. The Holy Spirit works in the Church to build her up, to bring her life, and to make her holy.

# Chapter 5 Activity:
# Finding God's Guidance in the Bible

- How did God help or challenge his people?

- How did God show that he was pleased (or displeased) with his people?

- What did God say or do to express how he wanted his people to live?

- In what section of the Bible do each of the following passages appear—the Pentateuch, the historical books, the wisdom and poetry books, or the prophets?

1. Genesis 1:26–31 (God creates)

2. Genesis 6:5–8, 9:8–15 (Noah)

3. Genesis 12:1–5 (Abraham)

4. Exodus 3:1–17 (Moses—I AM)

5. Exodus 13:20—14:30 (God parts the Red Sea)

6. Exodus 20:1–17 (the Ten Commandments)

7. Judges 2:11–19 (God sends judges)

8. 1 Samuel 8:1–22 (the people ask for a king)

9. 1 Samuel 16:1–3,8–13 (David is made a king)

10. 2 Kings 25:1–12 (destruction of the Temple)

11. Psalm 23:1–6 (The Lord is Our Shepherd)

12. Wisdom 6:1–11 (the responsibility of rulers)

13. Jeremiah 1:4–10 (call of the prophet Jeremiah)

14. Isaiah 52:13, 53:4–11 (God's Suffering Servant)

Document #: TX003505

# Chapter 6

## Creation

### Preparation and Supplies

- Study chapter 6, "Creation," in the handbook.
- Provide Bibles, one for each participant.
- Bring in a medium-sized rock.
- Provide a set of markers and a sheet of newsprint for each group of four or five.
- Make copies of the chapter 6 activity handout, "Recognizing God's Goodness" (Document #: TX003507), one for each participant. *(optional)*

### Pray It! (5 minutes)

**Tell** the participants that class will begin with a reading from Genesis. **Ask** a volunteer to read Genesis 1:27–31. **Direct** the young people to the Pray It! article on page 69 in the handbook. **Lead** them in saying the prayer together.

### Study It! (35 to 45 minutes, depending on your class length)

#### A. Why Does Evil Exist?

1. **Ask** the participants to guess how many hairs are on the average head and to write their guesses on a piece of scratch paper. **Ask** for a show of hands from those who guessed more than one million. **Continue** to narrow down the numbers until only the young people with the correct (or closest to the correct) answer have their hands raised. **Announce** that on average there are about 100,000 hairs on each person's head. **Comment** as follows in your own words:
   - ➢ Each one of us is unique, and although we may have different hair length, styles, or colors, Jesus says in Matthew 10:30, "As for you, even the hairs of your head have all been counted." This was Jesus' way of saying how important each person is to God, so important that he even keeps track of how many hairs are on our head.
   - ➢ If God keeps track of our hair, we all must be an important part of his creation.
2. **Direct** the participants to read the chapter introduction and the section "Why Does Evil Exist?," on pages 68–71 in the handbook. The content covers points 1 through 4 on the handout "Chapter 6 Summary" (Document #: TX003506).
3. *(Optional)* **Direct** the young people to the Think About It! article on page 70 in the handbook. **Invite** a volunteer to read the article aloud, and **use** the questions at the end to lead a discussion.

#### B. Sin

1. **Pick up** the medium-sized rock you brought to class and have the participants pass it around while you discuss the following questions with them:
   - ➢ Where did this rock come from? *(the ground)*
   - ➢ What is this rock made of? *(crystals of different kinds of minerals, or broken pieces of crystals)*
   - ➢ Where did the ingredients for the rock come from? *(Responses should lead to the answer "God made them.")*
   - ➢ In what ways could people use this rock? *(to make tools, to make weapons, to grind food, and so on)*
   - ➢ Is this rock good or bad? Explain why. *(Though people could use this rock for evil purposes, this rock is still part of God's creation, which makes it good.)*

2. **Direct** the participants to read the sections "Sin" and "The Journey of Creation," on pages 71–74 in the handbook. The content covers points 5 through 9 on the handout "Chapter 6 Summary" (Document #: TX003506).

3. *(Optional)* **Invite** the young people to share examples of ways they or someone they know has taken an aspect of God's creation and done something good with it.

## C. The Visible and the Invisible

**Direct** the participants to read the section "The Visible and the Invisible," on page 76 in the handbook. The content covers point 10 on the handout "Chapter 6 Summary" (Document #: TX003506). *Note:* If you are running short on time, you may wish to just briefly summarize this section.

## Live It! (15 to 20 minutes)

1. **Organize** the large group into groups of four or five and **distribute** a Bible to each participant. **Instruct** the young people to turn to Genesis 1:24—2:4 and read the passage silently. **Explain** the task as follows:

   ➢ Each group is to list at least five things the story tells us about God and creation that do not contradict what science tells us.

   ➢ Each group should choose a recorder to write down its ideas.

2. **Invite** each group to present its list to the large group. After each group has presented, **affirm** and **correct** their responses as necessary. **Include** the following comments if the group reports do not mention them:

   ➢ God created everything.

   ➢ God is all-powerful.

   ➢ Human beings are made in the image of God.

   ➢ Human beings are essentially good.

   ➢ All of creation is good.

   ➢ God shares his creative power with us.

   ➢ Humans are responsible to care for God's creation.

3. **Distribute** a set of markers and a sheet of newsprint to each group. **Ask** the participants to brainstorm how God's creative power can be found at work in the world today. **Invite** the groups to illustrate their examples on the newsprint. If they need some assistance, you might ask questions such as, "Where can you find people working to save lives?" or "What natural events help bring about new life?" When the groups have finished, **invite** each one to present its illustrations. **Use** the groups' examples to emphasize that God's creation continues.

## Optional Activity

**Distribute** the chapter 6 activity handout, "Recognizing God's Goodness" (Document #: TX003507), and **use** it to help the young people identify God's goodness in the world.

## Closing Prayer (5 minutes)

**Direct** the participants to the "Prayer of Saint Francis" on page 560 in the handbook. **Invite** them to take turns reading the lines of the prayer. **Close** with the Sign of the Cross.

## Online Resources

To access activities and a quiz related to this chapter, go to *www.smp.org/resourcecenter/books/* and click on "Catechist: Additional Course Handouts or Quizzes." Tip sheets and links are also available.

# Creation

## Chapter 6 Summary

### Chapter Learning Objectives

- The participants will explore God's creativity at work in our world.

- The participants will recognize their own unique place in God's plan and creation.

- The participants will examine the choice of human beings either to follow or to disobey God's plan for creation.

### Content Summary

1. God created the entire universe out of nothing and without help.

2. The role of science is to figure out the physical nature of the universe, but only God can reveal that creation is a gift of God's love.

3. Evil exists, but God's love continually turns evil into good.

4. In Jesus Christ, the Son of God, we see the triumph of good (the Resurrection) over evil (his suffering and death on the cross).

5. God created us in his image, as free and loving beings, so that we can freely choose between good and evil.

6. Sin is the choice of evil (even on a small scale) over good. Sin separates us, even in a small way, from God and from one another.

7. We can sin by omission—that is, by *not* doing something we know we should do.

8. The Word of God, Jesus Christ, became man to save us, to give us new life, and to restore and deepen our union with God.

9. God continually guides creation toward greater love, and, with the help of the Holy Spirit, we can cooperate with God in his plan.

10. In the Nicene Creed, we summarize what has been revealed about God and his plan for us, including the creation of the "invisible," the angels.

(All summary points are taken from *The Catholic Connections Handbook for Middle Schoolers, Second Edition.* Copyright © 2014 by Saint Mary's Press. All rights reserved.)

# Chapter 6 Activity: Recognizing God's Goodness

Have you ever noticed how news reports often feature bad news: natural disasters, crime, accidents, and so on? Even in your own life, you may sometimes feel like there's bad news all around. But the reality is that despite the challenges we all face and the negative events we might experience, the world is filled with God's goodness. On the lines below, list three examples of God's goodness in the world around you. Tell how each enriches your life.

| God's Goodness in the World | How This Makes My Life Better |
|---|---|
| 1. _____ | _____ |
| | _____ |
| 2. _____ | _____ |
| | _____ |
| 3. _____ | _____ |
| _____ | |

## People of Faith

Saint Francis of Assisi is known for his life of holiness and devotion to God. He is also known for the prayer for peace, called the "Prayer of Saint Francis." Quietly and reflectively, read the words of the prayer below. Choose two lines of the prayer and describe an example of how you might live each one in your everyday life.

Prayer lines I can live in my own life:

_____

_____

_____

How I can live them:

_____

_____

_____

_____

### Prayer of Saint Francis

*Lord, make me an instrument of your peace;*

*where there is hatred, let me sow love;*

*where there is injury, pardon;*

*where there is doubt, faith;*

*where there is despair, hope;*

*where there is darkness, light;*

*and where there is sadness, joy.*

*O Divine Master,*

*grant that I may not so much seek to be*
*    consoled as to console;*

*to be understood as to understand;*

*to be loved as to love.*

*For it is in giving that we receive,*

*it is in pardoning that we are pardoned,*

*and it is in dying that we are born to eternal life.*

Document #: TX003507

# Chapter 7
## The Human Person

### Preparation and Supplies

- Study chapter 7, "The Human Person," in the handbook.
- Provide Bibles, one for each participant.
- Provide a sheet of newsprint and markers, enough for each group of three or four.
- Make copies of the chapter 7 activity handout, "Humankind and Original Sin" (Document #: TX003509), one for each participant. *(optional)*

### Pray It! (5 minutes)

**Tell** the young people that the focus of this lesson is the human person—in other words . . . YOU! **Distribute** the Bibles and **ask** the participants to turn to Genesis 1:27–31 and mark it with their fingers. When all are ready, **ask** a volunteer to read the Scripture passage aloud. After the reading, **lead** the following prayer:

> ➤ Creator of all, we thank you for gathering all of us together today. Let each of us know how special we are to you. We are so happy that you love us, even though we are not perfect. We come here together to learn about who you made us to be. Even though we get lost sometimes, you are always there waiting and calling us back home. Amen.

### Study It! (40 to 50 minutes, depending on your class length)

#### A. Being Human

1. **Direct** the young people to turn to the picture of the sick child on page 78 in the handbook. **Lead** a discussion on the following question:
   > ➤ Why do bad things happen despite God's great love for us? *(In God's plan, good comes out of evil.)*

2. **Direct** the participants to read the chapter introduction and the section "Being Human," on pages 78–80 in the handbook. The content covers points 1 and 2 on the handout "Chapter 7 Summary" (Document #: TX003508).

3. *(Optional)* When the participants have finished the reading, **lead** a discussion on the following questions:
   > ➤ How did Steven's family's feelings change throughout his illness? *(At first they were angry and questioned how God could allow such a terrible thing to happen, but as people showed them so much kindness, they no longer felt angry. Instead, they became grateful to God for the help from so many good people.)*
   > ➤ Did something good come out of Steven's illness? What was it? *(Yes, the kindness that people showed Steven's family helped them to recognize God's goodness in the people who helped them. Perhaps in the future they will "pay it forward" and pass the kindness on to others.)*

## B. We Are Both, Not Just One

1. **Direct** the participants to the Think About It! article on page 82. **Invite** a volunteer to read the article aloud, and **use** the questions at the end to lead a discussion. *(Responses should reflect an understanding that our ability to love and care for others is a likeness of God, as is our free will. We can do things that are similar to what God does by caring for others and making choices that promote love and harmony.)*

2. **Direct** the young people to read the sections "Body and Soul" and "Original Sin," on pages 80–85 in the handbook. The content covers points 3 through 7 on the handout "Chapter 7 Summary" (Document #: TX003508).

3. *(Optional)* **Distribute** the chapter 7 activity handout, "Humankind and Original Sin" (Document #: TX003509), and **ask** the participants to complete the crossword puzzle.

## C. Coming from God, Heading toward God

**Direct** the participants to read the section, "Coming from God, Heading toward God," on pages 85–87 in the handbook. The content covers points 8 and 9 on the handout "Chapter 7 Summary" (Document #: TX003508).

*Note:* If you are running short on time, you may wish to just briefly summarize this section.

# Live It! (10 to 15 minutes)

1. **Organize** the young people into groups of three or four. **Distribute** a sheet of newsprint and a set of markers to each group. **Explain** the task as follows:
   - ➤ Each group is to draw an outline or a stick figure of a body on the sheet of newsprint. At the top of the newsprint, write "The Body of Christ."
   - ➤ Each group is now to write a phrase or draw a symbol of how young people can be the Body of Christ for others. Mark your group's ideas in the appropriate part on the body drawing. For example, you could write "helping a friend study for a test" on the head of the body, or you could write a math equation there. Another example would be writing "running in the 5K Muscular Dystrophy Fun Run" on the feet.

2. When the groups are done writing, **invite** each to present its newsprint to the large group. **Ask** the groups to briefly explain what they wrote on the newsprint.

3. **Comment** as follows in your own words:
   - ➤ Saint Teresa of Ávila wrote, "Christ has no body now but yours." This means that when we do God's will, our hands become the hands God uses to do his work.
   - ➤ Even though we have all been affected by Original Sin, we still have a choice to return to God. When we overcome temptation and choose to do God's will, we can live together as the Body of Christ that God destined us to be.

# Closing Prayer (5 minutes)

**Direct** the participants to turn to the Pray It! article on page 79 in the handbook. When all are ready, **invite** several young people to take turns slowly reading each line of the prayer in the article. **Close** with the Sign of the Cross.

# Online Resources

To access activities and a quiz related to this chapter, go to *www.smp.org/resourcecenter/books/* and click on "Catechist: Additional Course Handouts or Quizzes." Tip sheets and links are also available.

# The Human Person

## Chapter 7 Summary

### Chapter Learning Objectives

- The participants will explore what it means to be made in the image of God.

- The participants will examine how Original Sin affects every human being.

- The participants will express how we can live as the Body of Christ.

### Content Summary

1. Being human means that we are not God, and we are not perfect, but we are made in God's image.

2. We have the ability to love and care for one another.

3. We are made up of both a physical body and an immortal soul.

4. We are created male and female, with different gifts, so that we might learn to cooperate with one another.

5. We are made to love one another, especially in our families.

6. Original Sin, the sin committed by Adam and Eve, is the sinful condition into which all human beings, except Jesus (who is God and man) and his mother, Mary, are born. It is a loss of the freedom and holiness that God meant us to have. Even after Original Sin is washed away in Baptism, we are still affected by its consequences.

7. Original Sin makes it hard to say no to temptation—something that makes sinful things seem fun, exciting, or good to do.

8. We have come from God and, through Jesus Christ and his Church, we can return to God.

9. We can be like Christ by doing God's will—that is, choosing good and working for good in all circumstances.

# Chapter 7 Activity:
# Humankind and Original Sin

Complete the crossword puzzle.

**Across**

2. The name _____ comes from the Hebrew word for "life."

3. _____ Sin is the sin that our first parents committed, and the sinful condition that all people have from birth.

7. Original Sin affects every person except Jesus and _____.

9. A temptation makes something _____ seem fun or good to do.

**Down**

1. The Book of _____ contains two Creation stories.

4. Every human being is made in the _____ of God.

5. The name _____ comes from the Hebrew word for "man."

6. _____ is the model of the perfect human being.

8. All people are living beings made up of both a physical body and an immortal, _____.

# Chapter 8
# The Bible: Covenants

## Preparation and Supplies

- Study chapter 8, "The Bible: Covenants," in the handbook.
- Provide Bibles, one for each of four groups. *(optional)*
- Make copies of the chapter 8 activity handout, "Living the Ten Commandments" (Document #: TX003511), one for each group of two or three.

## Pray It! (5 minutes)

**Tell** the participants that class will begin with a reading from Scripture that describes God's covenant with Noah and the world. **Select** a volunteer to read Genesis 9:8–17. **Pray** the following:

> ➤ Lord, we are grateful that you saved us from our sins and gave us a chance to start over again. Every time we see a rainbow, let it remind us of your great love and mercy. May we always give to others the same love and forgiveness you have shown us. We ask this in Jesus' name. Amen.

## Study It! (40 to 50 minutes, depending on your class length)

### A. God Gives Second Chances

1. **Direct** the participants to find a partner and discuss a time when they were given a second chance. **Tell** them to describe the circumstances and how they reacted when they found out they were given a second chance. **Ask** volunteers to share their experiences.

2. **Direct** the young people to read the chapter introduction and the section "God Gives Second Chances," on pages 88–92 in the handbook. The content covers points 1 through 3 on the handout "Chapter 8 Summary" (Document #: TX003510).

3. *(Optional)* **Direct** the participants to the Think About It! article on page 94 in the handbook. **Use** the questions to lead a discussion.

### B. God's Covenants with Abraham, Moses, and David

1. **Direct** the young people to the "Fun Fact" article on page 92, and ask a volunteer to **read** the article aloud. **Tell** the participants that when they were baptized, the priest asked their parents what name they were giving their child. **Ask** volunteers to share the significance of the name they were given. Some maybe were named after a saint, after a grandparent, or after another significant person in their family. **Comment** as follows in your own words:

> ➤ Even if you don't know the significance of your name, your name is a symbol of the relationship that was established with God through Baptism. It is God's promise of salvation to you.

2. **Direct** the young people to read the section "God's Covenants with Abraham, Moses, and David," on pages 93–95 in the handbook. The content covers points 4 through 6 on the handout "Chapter 8 Summary" (Document #: TX003510).

3. *(Optional)* **Direct** the participants to the "Did You Know?" article on page 93 in the handbook. **Organize** the young people into four groups. **Distribute** a Bible to each group. **Assign** each group one of the Scripture passages listed in the article. **Ask** the groups to locate and read their passage in the Bible. **Tell** them to discuss the promise God makes in the reading and to whom. **Invite** volunteers from each group to share their findings.

## C. The New Covenant

**Direct** the participants to read the section "The New Covenant," on pages 96–97 in the handbook. The content covers points 7 through 9 on the handout "Chapter 8 Summary" (Document #: TX003510).

*Note:* If you are running short on time, you may wish to just briefly summarize this section.

## Live It! (10 to 15 minutes)

1. **Organize** the young people into groups of two or three. **Distribute** a copy of the chapter 8 activity handout, "Living the Ten Commandments" (Document #: TX003511), to each group. **Explain** the task as follows:
   ➤ The tablets listed on your handout contain the Ten Commandments, with an example of how to live several of them. In the empty spaces, each group is to explain what the commandment means.
2. After the groups have had time to complete the handout, **invite** volunteers from the groups to share their answers.
3. **Comment** as follows in your own words:
   ➤ In the covenant with Moses, God promises to be the God of the Chosen People, and to protect them. In turn, they promise to obey God's Law.
   ➤ The covenant fulfilled through Jesus Christ is called the New Covenant. It is really the fulfillment of the covenants God made with Noah, Abraham, Moses, and David.
   ➤ In the New Covenant, God promises salvation through his Son, Jesus Christ. Through the first Apostles and the Church today, this promise of salvation is preached to all, with the help of the Holy Spirit.
   ➤ When Christ returns, God's promise of salvation will be complete.

## Closing Prayer (5 minutes)

**Direct** the participants to the Pray It! article on page 89 in the handbook. **Lead** them in praying the prayer together. **Close** with the Sign of the Cross.

## Online Resources

To access activities and a quiz related to this chapter, go to *www.smp.org/resourcecenter/books/* and click on "Catechist: Additional Course Handouts or Quizzes." Tip sheets and links are also available.

# The Bible: Covenants

## Chapter 8 Summary

### Chapter Learning Objectives

- The participants will examine the covenants God made with human beings.

- The participants will examine how God's covenant with his people is fulfilled in Jesus Christ.

- The participants will reflect on how they can be faithful to God's Law today.

### Content Summary

1. God is faithful to his promises; therefore, we can trust him.

2. Covenants are promises made between God and human beings.

3. The covenant with Noah is the first covenant described in the Bible. The rainbow is identified as the symbol of that covenant.

4. In the covenant with Abraham, God promises to make Abraham's descendants a great people, and Abraham promises to be faithful to God.

5. In the covenant with Moses, God promises to be the God of the Chosen People and to protect them. In turn, they promise to obey God's Law.

6. In the covenant with David, God promises to establish David's throne forever. This covenant was fulfilled through Jesus Christ.

7. The covenant fulfilled through Jesus Christ is called the New Covenant. It is really the fulfillment of the covenants God made with Noah, Abraham, Moses, and David.

8. In the New Covenant, God promises salvation through his Son, Jesus Christ. Through the first Apostles and the Church today, this promise of salvation is preached to all, with the help of the Holy Spirit.

9. When Christ returns, God's promise of salvation will be complete.

# Chapter 8 Activity: Living the Ten Commandments

When God gave the Ten Commandments to Moses, he gave his Law to all people. The Ten Commandments give us a summary of how we are to live. The following tablets contain the Ten Commandments, with an example of how to live several of them. In the empty spaces, explain in your own words what each commandment means.

**Tablet 1**

1. I am the Lord your God. You shall not have other gods besides me.

2. You shall not take the name of the Lord, your God, in vain.

3. Remember to keep holy the Sabbath day.

4. Honor your father and mother.

5. You shall not kill.

6. You shall not commit adultery.

7. You shall not steal.

8. You shall not bear false witness against your neighbor.

9. You shall not covet your neighbor's wife.

10. You shall not covet anything that belongs to your neighbor.

**Tablet 2**

1. God is more important than anything else in our lives. We should not give material things excessive value.

2. Always speak God's name with respect.

3. _____

_____

4. _____

_____

5. Protect all human life and treat other people with the dignity they deserve.

6. We must respect our own bodies and the bodies of others.

7. _____

_____

8. _____

_____

9. We must show respect for others' sexuality in our thoughts, words, and actions.

10. _____

_____

Document #: TX003511

# Chapter 9
# Faith: Responding to God

## Preparation and Supplies

- Study chapter 9, "Faith: Responding to God," in the handbook.
- Provide two or three Bibles.
- Provide sheets of newsprint and sets of markers, enough for each group of three or four.
- Make copies of the chapter 9 activity handout, "Faithful to God" (Document #: TX003513), one for each participant.

## Pray It! (5 minutes)

**Tell** the participants that class will begin with a passage from Scripture that demonstrates the power of faith. **Ask** two or three volunteers to take turns reading Mark 9:17–24. After the reading, **direct** the young people to the Pray It! article on page 99 in the handbook. **Lead** them in praying the prayer together.

## Study It! (40 to 50 minutes, depending on your class length)

### A. What Is Faith?

1. **Ask** the participants to think of one thing they have done in the past week that would demonstrate their faith in God. **Invite** volunteers to share their action with the group. **Record** their answers on the board. (*Alternative:* Ask the young people to identify actions of people in the community who demonstrate faith in God, and then list those actions on the board.)
2. **Direct** the participants to read the chapter introduction and the sections "What Is Faith?" and "Faith Is a Gift Freely Chosen," on pages 98–101 in the handbook. The content covers points 1 through 3 on the handout "Chapter 9 Summary" (Document #: TX003512).
3. *(Optional)* Direct the participants to the Think About It! article on page 103 in the handbook. **Ask** a volunteer to read the article aloud. **Use** the questions in the article to engage the participants in a discussion on the challenges to, and questions about, our faith that we sometimes face.

### B. Faith Is Believing

1. **Write** the word *faith* on the board lengthwise so that each letter can serve as the beginning of a new word. **Tell** the participants to form pairs and together write down a phrase or sentence for each letter of the word *faith* that tells how you can put your faith into action. **Give** an example, such as "Follow the teachings of Jesus" for the letter *f*. After a few minutes, **ask** volunteers to share an answer for each letter, and **record** their phrases and sentences on the board.
2. **Direct** the young people to read the sections "Faith Is Believing," "Faith Is Trusting," and "Faith Is Doing," on pages 101–104 in the handbook. The content covers points 4 through 6 on the handout "Chapter 9 Summary" (Document #: TX003512).
3. *(Optional)* **Direct** the participants to the Live It! article on page 106 in the handbook. **Invite** a volunteer to read the article aloud. **Lead** a discussion by asking the following question:

> When it came to believing, trusting, and doing, what difficulties do you think Mother Teresa might have had to face?

**Ask** volunteers to share ways Mother Teresa's example inspires them and specific ways they can follow her example.

### C. Faith in God Alone

**Direct** the participants to read the section "Faith in God Alone," on pages 105–106 in the handbook. The content covers points 7 through 9 on the handout "Chapter 9 Summary" (Document #: TX003512).

*Note:* If you are running short on time, you may wish to just briefly summarize this section.

## Live It! (10 to 15 minutes)

1. **Organize** the large group into groups of three or four. **Distribute** a sheet of newsprint and a set of markers to each group. **Explain** the task as follows:
   > Each group will have 3 to 5 minutes to draw or list all the ways they rely on other people or things to make them secure or happy.
2. After the 3 to 5 minutes are up, **ask** the groups to review their drawings and lists and explain to the large group why each of these things will not make them happy or secure. **Emphasize** that the happiness about which you are speaking is not the temporary fulfillment that something new might bring. To make this point, **ask** the participants to recall some of their old discarded belongings and toys that they once could not live without.
3. **Comment** as follows in your own words:
   > Although many things make us happy for a short time, only by knowing God will we ever be truly happy.
   > Material things come and go. You might have a lot one day and very little the next. If your happiness relies on having things, then your happiness can be taken away or lost.
   > Having faith in God cannot be taken away by anyone else. It is what your eternal salvation depends on. When you die, God will not ask you how much money you made.
   > There is only one true God on whom we can rely. Only God can provide us with the kind of happiness that cannot be taken away.

## Optional Activity

**Use** the chapter 9 activity handout, "Faithful to God" (Document #: TX003513), to help the participants identify distractions from their faith in God and how they can overcome those distractions.

## Closing Prayer (5 minutes)

**Instruct** the participants to turn to page 559 and **lead** them in praying the Nicene Creed together. **Close** with the Sign of the Cross.

## Online Resources

To access activities and a quiz related to this chapter, go to *www.smp.org/resourcecenter/books/* and click on "Catechist: Additional Course Handouts or Quizzes." Tip sheets and links are also available.

# Faith: Responding to God

## Chapter 9 Summary

### Chapter Learning Objectives

- The participants will examine faith as a gift from God that we can choose whether to accept.

- The participants will explore faith in the three elements of believing, trusting, and doing.

- The participants will reflect on the happiness and security that only God can provide.

### Content Summary

1. Faith is believing in God, but it is also accepting that God made himself known through Jesus Christ, and living our lives based on that belief.

2. Faith is entrusting our lives to God.

3. Faith is a gift from God, yet it is also a choice we make.

4. We express our faith when we proclaim the Nicene Creed. Faith is an individual response to God, and also an act of the entire Church.

5. Faith is built on belief and leads to trust. In faith we allow God to guide our lives, leading to joy and happiness in this life and in the next.

6. Faith means acting on what we believe and doing small things with great love.

7. Faith means believing in one God, and allowing nothing else to take the place of God in our lives.

8. We have come from God and, through Jesus Christ and his Church, we can return to God.

9. We can be like Christ by doing God's will—that is, choosing good and working for good in all circumstances.

# Chapter 9 Activity: Faithful to God

It can be difficult to live in the modern world and remain faithful to God's will. What are three things in your life that distract you from your faith in God and from following his will? List them in the left-hand column below. In the right-hand column, describe what you can do to overcome each of these distractions.

| Distractions from my faith in God | How I can overcome them |
|---|---|
| **1** _____ <br> _____ <br> _____ <br> _____ | _____ <br> _____ <br> _____ <br> _____ |
| **2** _____ <br> _____ <br> _____ <br> _____ | _____ <br> _____ <br> _____ <br> _____ |
| **3** _____ <br> _____ <br> _____ <br> _____ | _____ <br> _____ <br> _____ <br> _____ |

Document #: TX003513

# Chapter 10

## The Bible: The Prophets

### Preparation and Supplies

- Study chapter 10, "The Bible: The Prophets," in the handbook.
- Provide a Bible.
- Gather a variety of magazines and newspapers, newsprint, glue, and markers, enough for each group of three or four.
- Make copies of the chapter 10 activity handout, "Live It!" (Document #: TX003515), one for each participant. *(optional)*

### Pray It! (5 minutes)

**Tell** the participants that class will begin with a reading from Scripture in which God calls Jeremiah to be a prophet to his people. **Invite** a volunteer to read Jeremiah 1:4–10. **Pray** the following:

> ➤ Lord, you call each of us to follow you and spread your message, even though we may think we are too young or inexperienced. Your plan for us was in place even before we were born. Help us to understand your will for us and to follow your call. Give us the courage to spread your message of love to all people. Amen.

### Study It! (35 to 45 minutes, depending on your class length)

#### A. The Non-Writing Prophets

1. **Brainstorm** with the participants bad situations that young people their age are often pressured into by their peers. **Offer** some examples, such as shoplifting, skipping school, or telling lies to their parents about where they are going. **Record** the participants' responses on the board. **Ask** what kind of qualities they would want in a friend if they were starting down a wrong path in life. **Record** the list of qualities on the board as well.

2. **Direct** the participants to read the chapter introduction and the section "The Non-Writing Prophets," on pages 108–112 in the handbook. The content covers points 1 through 3 on the handout "Chapter 10 Summary" (Document #: TX003514).

3. *(Optional)* **Direct** the young people to the Think About It! article on page 116 in the handbook. **Ask** a volunteer to read the article aloud, and **use** the questions at the end to lead a discussion.

#### B. The Classical Prophets

1. **Arrange** the large group by gender. **Ask** each group to brainstorm a list of talents and gifts their gender brings to the mission of the Church. **Ask** both groups to create a list of the gifts the opposite gender contributes. **Invite** each group to share its list. **Point out** any similarities and differences.

2. **Direct** the participants to read the section "The Classical Prophets," on pages 113–116 in the handbook. The content covers points 4 and 5 on the handout "Chapter 10 Summary" (Document #: TX003514).

3. **(Optional) Direct** the young people to the Live It! article on page 111 in the handbook. **Read** the article. **Ask** the participants to find a partner and answer the questions at the end of the article. **Invite** volunteers to share their answers with the large group.

## C. The Hope for a Messiah

**Direct** the participants to read the section "The Hope for a Messiah," on pages 116–118 in the handbook. The content covers points 6 through 8 on the handout "Chapter 10 Summary" (Document #: TX003514).

*Note:* If you are running short on time, you may wish to just briefly summarize this section.

## Live It! (15 to 20 minutes)

1. **Organize** the young people into groups of three or four. **Distribute** a variety of magazines and newspapers, a sheet of newsprint, glue, and markers to each group. **Explain** the task as follows:
   - ➢ Each group is to look through the newspapers and magazines it has been given to find a situation from our contemporary world that may be in need of a prophet.
   - ➢ Each group will then have the opportunity to assume the role of prophet and write a prophecy dealing with the situation the group has chosen.
   - ➢ In writing your group's prophecy, consider the following questions:
     - • What would God want his spokesperson to say about this situation?
     - • How would God's Word challenge that particular group of people?
   - ➢ Be specific in your prophecy and be sure to include both consequences if the Word of God is ignored and the promised blessings if they heed God's Word.
   - ➢ Select a person from your group to record your prophecy on the newsprint.
2. **Invite** a representative from each group to share the group's contemporary situation and prophecy with the entire group.
3. **Comment** as follows in your own words:
   - ➢ The prophets faithfully spoke God's Word to God's people.
   - ➢ God sent prophets to his people to remind them to keep their covenant with him.
   - ➢ The prophets prepared God's people for the coming of the Messiah. These prophecies were fulfilled in Jesus Christ.
   - ➢ By virtue of our Baptism, we are called to participate in the priestly, prophetic, and kingly ministry of Christ— in other words, to share the Good News with the world.

10

## Optional Activity

Use the chapter 10 activity handout, "Live It!" (Document #: TX003515), to help the participants explore ways they can spread God's message to others.

## Closing Prayer (5 minutes)

**Direct** the participants to the Pray It! article on page 109 in the handbook. **Ask** a few volunteers to take turns reading the lines of the prayer. **Close** with the Sign of the Cross.

## Online Resources

To access activities and a quiz related to this chapter, go to *www.smp.org/resourcecenter/books/* and click on "Catechist: Additional Course Handouts or Quizzes." Tip sheets and links are also available.

# The Bible: The Prophets

## Chapter 10 Summary

### Chapter Learning Objectives

- The participants will explore the role of prophets in God's plan for salvation.

- The participants will examine how the message of the prophets was fulfilled in Jesus Christ.

- The participants will reflect on their own call to spread God's message.

### Content Summary

1. The prophets faithfully spoke God's Word to God's people.

2. God sent prophets to his people to remind them to keep their covenant with him.

3. Two famous non-writing prophets were Elijah and Elisha. Elisha was Elijah's helper and took on Elijah's role as prophet after Elijah was taken up to Heaven.

4. The writing prophets are also called the classical prophets. These are divided into major prophets and minor prophets.

5. Amos is an example of a minor prophet and Ezekiel is an example of a major prophet.

6. The prophets prepared God's people for the coming of the Messiah.

7. Isaiah is a major prophet whose words and the words of his later followers are found in three sections of the Book of Isaiah—First Isaiah, Second Isaiah, and Third Isaiah.

8. The prophecies of Isaiah about the Messiah were fulfilled in Jesus Christ.

# Chapter 10 Activity: Live It!

There are many ways to reveal God's Word to others. Sometimes we do so through our words, other times through our actions. On the lines below, list three ways you can reveal God's Word to others through your words, and three ways you can do so through your actions.

| Through My Words | Through My Actions |
| --- | --- |
| _____ | _____ |
| _____ | _____ |
| _____ | _____ |

Imagine that you are telling a friend who is not a Christian why you are a follower of Jesus. What are the two most important things you would share?

_____

_____

_____

_____

_____

_____

_____

_____

Document #: TX003515

# Chapter 11
# Jesus Christ, True God and True Man

## Preparation and Supplies

- Study chapter 11, "Jesus Christ, True God and True Man," in the handbook.
- Provide a Bible, one for each group.
- Prepare slips of paper, one for each group, each with one of the following Scripture citations written on it:
  - Matthew 1:18–23
  - Mark 9:7
  - Luke 3:21
  - John 1:14
  - John 8:58
  - John 10:30
  - Philippians 2:6–7
- Make copies of the chapter 11 activity handout, "Jesus Christ, True God and True Man" (Document #: TX003517), one for each participant. *(optional)*

## Pray It! (5 minutes)

**Tell** the participants that this lesson will explore the importance of relationships with Jesus and with one another. **Invite** a volunteer to read John 1:1–5. **Pray** the following:

> ➤ Creator God, we stand before you today with open hearts and minds, seeking to know more about your Son, Jesus. Through Sacred Scripture and Sacred Tradition, help us to truly know you, Lord. Amen.

## Study It! (40 to 50 minutes, depending on your class length)

### A. Who Is Jesus Christ?

1. **Invite** a volunteer to be interviewed by the group. **Ask** the volunteer to step out for just a moment. While she or he is gone, **explain** to the participants that they will be asking the volunteer only one question, over and over again: "Who are you?" They can ask the question using a funny voice or in another language, but they should ask only the question "Who are you?" **Call** the volunteer back. **Explain** the volunteer's task as follows:

   > ➤ Your job is to call on participants who have questions to ask you. You must answer the questions truthfully, but you must give a different answer each time.

   **Allow** five to ten young people to ask the question. **Record** the volunteer's answers on the board. When the questioning is complete, **ask** the participants to review the answers and identify the categories used to answer the question "Who are you?" **Ask** the young people to add any other categories that would give us clues about who a person is. (Answers should include name, origin, birthplace, age, family members, friends, titles, occupation, residence, religion, gender, nationality, education, hobbies.)

2. **Direct** the participants to read the chapter introduction and the section "Who Is Jesus Christ?" on pages 120–125 in the handbook. The content covers points 1 through 5 on the handout "Chapter 11 Summary" (Document #: TX003516).

3. *(Optional)* **Direct** the young people to the "Did You Know?" article on page 135 in the handbook. **Ask** a volunteer to read the article aloud. **Lead** a discussion exploring the reasons why it was not easy for the Jewish people to accept that Jesus is God.

## B. What the Incarnation Means for Us

1. **Organize** the participants into five groups. **Direct** the groups to the image on page 128 in the handbook. **Assign** each group a different word (Savior, Mediator, Friend, Teacher, Model) to describe who Jesus is. **Ask** each group to describe in writing how Jesus is Savior, Mediator, and so on, for them. **Invite** the groups to share their responses with the large group.

2. **Direct** the young people to read the section "What the Incarnation Means for Us," on pages 125–129 in the handbook. The content covers points 6 through 10 on the handout "Chapter 11 Summary" (Document #: TX003516).

3. *(Optional)* **Direct** the participants to the Think About It! article on page 126 in the handbook. **Invite** volunteers to respond to the questions. **Share** with the class your own responses. See Matthew 25:31–46 and Matthew 18:21–23 for examples.

## Live It! (10 to 15 minutes)

1. **Divide** the large group into groups of two or three. **Distribute** to each group a Bible and a slip of paper with a Scripture passage written on it. **Explain** the task as follows:
   ➢ Each group is to locate and read the passage and then try to figure out how it answers the "Who are you?" question about Jesus.
   ➢ Each group should record its answers on a sheet of paper and select a person from their group to share with the large group.

2. **Invite** the representative from each group to read his or her group's Scripture passage and to share the group's responses.

3. **Comment** as follows in your own words:
   ➢ We get to know Jesus Christ through Sacred Scripture and the Tradition of the Church. The names and title for Jesus, his family, his ancestors, and other aspects of Jesus' life teach us a great deal about who Jesus is.
   ➢ Jesus Christ is one Divine Person with two natures: a human nature and a divine nature. He is both fully divine and fully human. He is like us in all things but sin. This is the mystery of the Incarnation.
   ➢ Jesus is our teacher. Not only can we imitate him and follow him but, through Baptism and the other Sacraments, we are also given the power of his life, a power of relationship that we call *grace*. We can live like Jesus, love like Jesus, become like Jesus. We can share in his glory now and forever.

## Optional Activity

**Distribute** to each young person a copy of the chapter 11 activity handout, "Jesus Christ, True God and True Man" (Document #: TX003517), to help the participants examine their own relationship with Jesus and their understanding of the Incarnation.

## Closing Prayer (5 minutes)

**Direct** the participants to the Pray It! article on page 121 in the handbook. **Ask** a volunteer to read the prayer aloud. **Close** with the Sign of the Cross.

## Online Resources

To access activities and a quiz related to this chapter, go to *www.smp.org/resourcecenter/books/* and click on "Catechist: Additional Course Handouts or Quizzes." Tip sheets and links are also available.

# Jesus Christ, True God and True Man

## Chapter 11 Summary

### Chapter Learning Objectives

- The participants will explore the question "Who are you?" in relation to one another and Jesus.

- The participants will learn that Jesus is fully God and fully man.

- The participants will examine the many different ways we learn about who Jesus is, particularly through Sacred Scripture and Sacred Tradition.

### Content Summary

1. The mystery of the Incarnation is the truth that Jesus Christ, the Son of God and the Second Person of the Trinity, is both fully God and fully man.

2. Jesus wants to give us the power to become like him so that he lives through us.

3. We get to know Jesus Christ through Sacred Scripture and the Sacred Tradition of the Church.

4. Jesus Christ is one Divine Person with two natures: a human nature and a divine nature. He is both fully divine and fully human. He is like us in all things but sin.

5. Jesus is truly God because he is one with God and does things only God can do.

6. Jesus is truly the Messiah, the "anointed one" sent by God to be our priest, prophet, and king.

7. The name *Jesus* means "God saves." The primary mission of Jesus is to save us from sin and death through the divine life of God (that is, grace).

8. Jesus, as both God and man, is the one and perfect mediator between us and God.

9. Jesus understands us perfectly and wants to be our friend.

10. Jesus is our teacher. Not only can we imitate him and follow him but, through Baptism and the other Sacraments, we are given the power of his life. We can live like Jesus, love like Jesus, become like Jesus. We can share in his glory now and forever.

# Chapter 11 Activity: Jesus Christ, True God and True Man

Recall times when you received unexpected good news, either of an everyday nature—such as getting a better grade than you expected on a test—or on a far bigger, perhaps life-changing, scale. Describe an example of each of these types of events.

_____

_____

_____

_____

How is the Good News of the birth of Jesus life-changing Good News for all people?

_____

_____

_____

As the second Person of the Blessed Trinity, Jesus is God. Yet through the Incarnation, his birth, Jesus also became truly man. How does Jesus' human nature and his experience of human emotions and suffering affect the way you relate to him?

_____

_____

_____

Document #: TX003517

# Chapter 12

## The Birth of Jesus

### Preparation and Supplies

- Study chapter 12, "The Birth of Jesus," in the handbook.
- Provide a Bible.
- Gather sheets of newsprint and sets of markers, enough for each of four or five groups.
- Make copies of the chapter 12 activity handout, "Who Am I?" (Document #: TX003519), one for each participant. *(optional)*

### Pray It! (5 minutes)

**Tell** the participants that class will begin with a reading from Scripture that tells of the birth of Jesus. **Invite** a volunteer to read Luke 2:1–7. **Direct** the participants to turn to the Pray It! article on page 131 in the handbook. **Lead** them in praying the prayer together.

### Study It! (35 to 45 minutes, depending on your class length)

#### A. The Birth of Jesus

1. **Ask** the participants to share some ways their families celebrate the coming of Christ at Christmas. **Record** the responses on the board.
2. **Direct** the participants to read the chapter introduction on pages 130–133 in the handbook. The content covers points 1 through 4 on the handout "Chapter 12 Summary" (Document #: TX003518).
3. *(Optional)* **Direct** the participants to the Think About It! article on page 133 in the handbook. **Ask** a volunteer to read the article aloud, and **use** the question at the end to lead a discussion.

#### B. Mary, the Mother of Jesus

1. **Invite** a volunteer to read Luke 1:26–38. **Ask** the participants to brainstorm ways that Mary is an inspiration and a source of encouragement for all Christians. **Review** points 5 and 7 through 10 on the handout "Chapter 12 Summary" (Document #: TX003518).
2. **Direct** the young people to read the section "Mary, the Mother of Jesus," on pages 133–135 in the handbook. The content covers points 5 through 8 on the handout "Chapter 12 Summary" (Document #: TX003518).
3. *(Optional)* **Direct** the participants to the illustration on page 136 in the handbook, and **use** the statement to lead a discussion about ways to appreciate and cultivate inner beauty in ourselves and others.

#### C. Mary's Example

**Direct** the participants to read the section "Mary's Example," on pages 135–136 in the handbook. The content covers points 9 and 10 on the handout "Chapter 12 Summary" (Document #: TX003518).

*Note:* If you are running short on time, you may wish to just briefly summarize this section.

# Live It! (15 to 20 minutes)

1. **Organize** the young people into four or five groups. **Distribute** a sheet of newsprint and a set of markers to each group. **Explain** the task as follows:

   ➢ Each group is to design a poster announcing the birth of Jesus. Add artwork and words to your poster to communicate your message. Be sure to include sacred artwork and text on your poster. Choose a Scripture quote from chapter 12 in the handbook to include at the bottom of the poster.

2. When the groups are ready, **invite** them to present their posters to the large group and to explain the message they are trying to communicate.

3. **Comment** as follows in your own words:

   ➢ We find the accounts of Jesus' birth in the Gospels of Matthew and Luke. The Son of God chose to be born in the poorest of circumstances. From this we can learn not to judge or value others based on their social status, material possessions, or appearance.

   ➢ In the Gospel of Matthew, the Magi, the wise men from the East, visit Jesus and worship him. This reminds us that Christ has come to all people.

   ➢ In the Gospel of Matthew, Jesus escapes from the decree of Herod just as Moses escaped from the decree of the Pharaoh. In this way, Matthew shows us that Jesus is like the great leaders of the Old Testament and is the Savior promised by God.

# Optional Activity

**Distribute** to each participant a copy of the chapter 12 activity handout, "Who Am I?" (Document #: TX003519), and ask the young people to complete it to reinforce the lesson.

# Closing Prayer (5 minutes)

**Direct** the participants to page 557 in the handbook. **Lead** them in praying the Hail Mary together. **Close** with the Sign of the Cross.

# Online Resources

To access activities and a quiz related to this chapter, go to *www.smp.org/resourcecenter/books/* and click on "Catechist: Additional Course Handouts or Quizzes." Tip sheets and links are also available.

# The Birth of Jesus
## Chapter 12 Summary

## Chapter Learning Objectives

- The participants will reflect on their experience and understanding of the celebration of Christmas.

- The participants will examine Jesus' birth and how it brings hope to all people.

- The participants will explore Mary's role in God's plan for our salvation.

## Content Summary

1. The Annunciation is the announcement of the angel Gabriel to Mary that she had been chosen by God to be the mother of his Son.

2. We find the accounts of Jesus' birth in the Gospels of Matthew and Luke. The Son of God chose to be born in the poorest of circumstances. From this we learn not to judge or value others based on their social status, material possessions, or appearance.

3. In the Gospel of Matthew, the Magi, the wise men from the East, visit Jesus and worship him. This reminds us that Christ has come to all people.

4. In the Gospel of Matthew, Jesus escapes from the decree of Herod just as Moses escaped from the decree of the Pharaoh. In this way, Matthew shows us that Jesus is like the great leaders of the Old Testament and is the Savior promised by God.

5. Mary is the Mother of God because Jesus is both God and man. She is the Mother of the Church because the Church is the Body of Christ. She is our spiritual mother and leads us to her son, Jesus.

6. Jesus is truly the Messiah, the "anointed one" sent by God to be our priest, prophet, and king.

7. Mary, although she is human like us, was preserved from Original Sin from the time of her conception. We call this fact the Immaculate Conception. Mary also remained pure from all personal sin throughout her life.

8. Mary remained a virgin, even though she gave birth to a child. Yet she was also married to Joseph. Having lived an ordinary life, she is an example for all people who follow God's ways.

9. Mary was closely united to Jesus in his act of redemption. She freely obeyed God's desire without complaint. As Jesus is the New Adam, so Mary is the New Eve, obedient to God's plan.

10. Mary is humble. She knows her great gifts come from God. In her service to others, she encourages us to be grateful for God's gifts to us and to live in faithfulness to God.

# Chapter 12 Activity: Who Am I?

Identify the person or persons described in each clue. More than one clue can describe the same person.

1. God chose me to be the mother of his Son.

_____

2. We traveled a long distance, guided by a strange star, to greet the newborn King of the Jews.

_____

3. We were not able to find a place to stay on the night Jesus was born.

_____

4. I was free from Original Sin from the moment of my conception, a fact called the Immaculate Conception, and remained free from personal sin throughout my life.

_____

5. I am the second Divine Person of the Trinity.

_____

6. I was a fourth-century bishop whose generosity led to the custom of giving gifts in my name at Christmas.

_____

7. It is through my power that the Virgin Mary conceived Jesus.

_____

8. I appeared to the Virgin Mary to ask her to be the mother of Jesus.

_____

9. Upon hearing of the birth of Jesus, I gave orders to kill all the boys in Bethlehem.

_____

10. Even though I am the Son of God, I was born in a stable, where a manger served as my cradle.

_____

Document #: TX003519

# Chapter 13

## Jesus Teaches

### Preparation and Supplies

- Study chapter 13, "Jesus Teaches," in the handbook.
- Make copies of the chapter 13 activity handout, "Picturing the Kingdom of God" (Document #: TX003521), one for each participant.
- Provide Bibles, one for each group, or one for each participant if possible.

### Pray It! (5 minutes)

**Tell** the participants that class will begin with a reading from Jesus' teachings in Scripture. **Ask** a volunteer to read Matthew 5:13–16. Pray the following:

> ➢ Lord Jesus, guide us today as we explore your teachings, and give us courage to allow your light to shine brightly through us as individuals and as a Christian community. Amen.

### Study It! (35 to 45 minutes, depending on your class length)

#### A. The Kingdom of God

1. **Distribute** the chapter 13 activity handout, "Picturing the Kingdom of God" (Document #: TX003521), to each young person. **Direct** the participants to complete the activity. When they are finished, **invite** volunteers to share their vision of what God's Kingdom will be like. **Engage** the young people in a discussion about which images occur most frequently in the descriptions. **Invite** volunteers to share their responses to the second part of the activity. **Ask** volunteers to explain why the positive qualities might be an essential part of the Kingdom of God.

2. **Direct** the participants to read the chapter introduction and the section "The Kingdom of God," on pages 138–139 in the handbook. The content covers points 1 through 4 on the handout "Chapter 13 Summary" (Document #: TX003520).

3. *(Optional)* **Direct** the young people to the Live It! article on page 143 in the handbook. **Ask** a volunteer to read the article aloud, and have the participants brainstorm everyday things young people their age can do to be "prophets" leading others to God's Kingdom.

#### B. Jesus Teaches in His Hidden Life

1. **Direct** the participants to the illustration of Jesus as a teacher on page 142 in the handbook. **Use** the question to brainstorm with the young people ways Jesus taught his followers.

2. **Direct** the participants to read the sections "Jesus Teaches in His Hidden Life" and "Jesus Teaches in Public Life," on pages 140–146 in the handbook. The content covers points 5 through 10 on the handout "Chapter 13 Summary" (Document #: TX003520).

3. *(Optional)* **Ask** a volunteer to read aloud "The Church's Teaching" in the Church History article on page 149 in the handbook. Emphasize the message in the last paragraph. **Invite** the

young people to share predictions they have heard about the end of the world, and when or how this would happen. **Explain** the following:

> Although such predictions can be entertaining or make good plots for a movie, in reality no one knows when or how the world will end. Our most important focus should be living every day as true followers of Jesus and leading a good moral life, faithful to God.

### C. Jesus and the Law

**Direct** the participants to read the section "Jesus and the Law," on pages 146–148 in the handbook. The content covers points 11 and 12 on the handout "Chapter 13 Summary" (Document #: TX003520).

*Note:* If you are running short on time, you may wish to just briefly summarize this section.

## Live It! (15 to 20 minutes)

1. **Organize** the young people into groups of three or four. **Assign** each group one of the parables from the list on page 145 in the handbook. **Ask** each group to choose a spokesperson. **Explain** the task as follows:

> Each group is to read its assigned parable in the Bible, and to plan a skit based on the parable that the group will perform for the rest of the class.

> In addition to acting out the parable, each group is to share with the rest of the class what the parable means for us today, especially for young people your age.

2. After the groups have had sufficient time, **invite** each to come forward and present its skit, beginning with the spokesperson's announcing the title of the parable. After the group performs the skit, have the spokesperson lead the group's presentation about the meaning of the parable for the modern world.

3. **Comment** as follows in your own words:

> During his public life, Jesus both talks about the Kingdom and begins to bring it about. He gathers followers and prepares them for his death and Resurrection.

> Jesus teaches that all who have the faith and humility to accept his words are welcome in the Kingdom of God.

> Jesus teaches through parables—stories that help his listeners make comparisons between their lives and the events told in the story.

## Closing Prayer (5 minutes)

**Direct** the participants to the Pray It! article on page 139. **Invite** a volunteer to read the prayer. **Conclude** with the following:

> Lord, open our minds to the wisdom of your Word. Let your example and teachings form us and guide us as we continue on our lifelong journey of learning. Amen.

**Close** with the Sign of the Cross.

## Online Resources

To access activities and a quiz related to this chapter, go to *www.smp.org/resourcecenter/books/* and click on "Catechist: Additional Course Handouts or Quizzes." Tip sheets and links are also available.

# Jesus Teaches

## Chapter 13 Summary

### Chapter Learning Objectives

- The participants will examine Jesus' private and public life and how each can teach us how to live as members of God's Kingdom.

- The participants will explore Jesus' parables and the lessons Jesus teaches through them.

### Content Summary

1. Jesus Christ, the Son of God, came in person to reclaim God's Kingdom and break the devil's power.

2. The Kingdom of God is not a specific place, but starts in our hearts. It is made real when we live God's rule of love and goodness.

3. Jesus not only tells us but also shows us how to live as a seed of the Kingdom.

4. All of Jesus' life teaches us—both his hidden life and his public life.

5. The hidden life of Jesus teaches us that an ordinary life, lived well with God and others, has great worth.

6. The events of Jesus' life teach us how to live—to be humble, to accept the suffering that comes to us, to respect legitimate authority, to do honest work.

7. During his public life, Jesus both talks about the Kingdom and begins to bring it about. He gathers followers and prepares them for his death and Resurrection.

8. Jesus teaches that all who have the faith and humility to accept his words are welcome in the Kingdom of God.

9. Jesus teaches through parables—stories that help his listeners make comparisons between their lives and the events told in the story.

10. In the Transfiguration, Jesus gives three Apostles (Peter, James, and John) a special view of the Kingdom of God. Jesus' appearance was transformed, and the Father's voice was heard, announcing his approval of his Son.

11. In his teaching, Jesus affirmed the Law of Moses, yet also made clear the bigger picture of living the Law in the Kingdom of God with a purer love.

12. Jesus also rejected some of the ways that Jewish teachers explained the Law. Jesus focused on the importance of love above man-made rules. Through his death and Resurrection, he showed the depths of his love, and then sent the Holy Spirit to us so that we too might live freely as God's children in his Kingdom.

# Chapter 13 Activity:
# Picturing the Kingdom of God

In Sacred Scripture, Jesus teaches about the Kingdom of God. Although the Kingdom of God will reach its fullness in Heaven, we can strive to build it on earth. On the lines below, describe what you imagine the Kingdom of God on earth to be like. Be sure to include details about how people who are part of it would live.

_____

_____

_____

_____

To live as Kingdom people, we must have certain qualities that are in keeping with Jesus' teachings. In the list below, circle those qualities or habits that a follower of Jesus must have. Choose two qualities that you circled and explain how you can grow in them.

| | |
|---|---|
| kindness | truthfulness |
| prayerfulness | service to others |
| gossiping | compassion |
| generosity | trust in God |
| jealousy | materialism |

**Two qualities I will strive to grow in:**_____

_____

**How I will do so:**_____

_____

_____

_____

Document #: TX003521

# Chapter 14

# Jesus Heals

## Preparation and Supplies

- Study chapter 14, "Jesus Heals," in the handbook.
- Provide Bibles, one for each group.
- Write the following questions on the board:
  - What is your superhero's name?
  - Why is this your favorite superhero?
  - What superpowers does your superhero have?
- Make copies of the chapter 14 activity handout, "Jesus Heals" (Document #: TX003523), one for each participant. *(optional)*

## Pray It! (5 minutes)

**Tell** the participants that class will begin with a prayer for healing. **Ask** a volunteer to read Mark 10:46–52. **Pray** the following:

> ➤ Lord, we call out to you for healing in our lives and in the lives of those we love. We trust in your mercy and kindness. Fill us with a spirit of compassion so that we may bring your healing to others who are in need. Amen.

**Close** with the Sign of the Cross.

## Study It! (40 to 50 minutes, depending on your class length)

### A. Jesus Heals the Body

1. **Ask** the young people to take out a sheet of paper and draw a picture of their favorite superhero. When they have finished their drawings, **ask** them to find a partner and discuss together the heroes they've drawn, using the questions on the board as a guide.

   After a few minutes, **share** the following points in your own words:

   > ➤ The superheroes we read about in comics and watch on television and in the movies are imaginary. Jesus Christ is real, and his power to perform miracles was and continues to be real. Yet he always taught that all of us are called to be heroes by serving others. Like Jesus we are called to love and serve others, not for our own gain but to share God's love.

2. **Direct** the participants to read the chapter introduction and the section "Jesus Heals the Body," on pages 150–153 in the handbook. The content covers points 1 through 5 on the handout "Chapter 14 Summary" (Document #: TX003522).

3. *(Optional)* **Direct** the young people to the Think About It! article on page 153 in the handbook. **Invite** a volunteer to read the article aloud, and **use** the question at the end to lead a discussion.

### B. Jesus Heals the Soul

1. **Create** three wide columns on the board and **label** them with the following heads: "World," "Country," "Local Community." **Arrange** the participants into three groups of equal size. **Assign** each group one of the three headings. **Explain** the task as follows:

   > ➤ Each group will compete in a relay race. The three groups will gather in the back of the classroom, and when I say "Go!" one person from each group will run to the board and write in the appropriate column a way to bring healing to his or her

assigned group. After writing the idea, the student must run back and tag the hand of the next person on his or her team, and then that person will run to the board. The team that comes up with the most ideas for healing is the winner.

(*Note:* **Encourage** ambitious but realistic changes, like ending world hunger, as opposed to fantastical ones, like changing human beings so we can survive by eating paper.)

2. **Direct** the young people to read the section "Jesus Heals the Soul," on pages 153–157 in the handbook. The content covers points 6 through 9 on the handout "Chapter 14 Summary" (Document #: TX003522).

3. *(Optional)* **Direct** the participants to the Did You Know? article on page 160 in the handbook. **Ask** a volunteer to read the article aloud, and then **draw** a comparison between the effect the Apostles' cures had on those who experienced or witnessed them and the effect our good works might have on others.

## C. Jesus Sends Us to Heal

**Direct** the participants to read the section "Jesus Sends Us to Heal," on pages 158–160 in the handbook. The content covers points 10 through 12 on the handout "Chapter 14 Summary" (Document #: TX003522).

*Note:* If you are running short on time, you may wish to just briefly summarize this section.

# Live It! (10 to 15 minutes)

1. **Organize** the young people into four or five groups. **Distribute** a Bible to each group, and **ask** each group to choose one person to be the note taker and spokesperson. **Assign** each group one of Jesus' miracles from the list on page 154 in the handbook. **Explain** as follows:
   ➤ Each group is to read its assigned miracle in the Bible and then summarize the following information about the miracle: *Who* are the main characters? *What* happened? *When* did the miracle happen? *How* did Jesus perform the miracle?

2. When everyone has finished, **invite** the spokesperson for each group to come forward and share the report with the large group.

3. **Comment** as follows in your own words:
   ➤ In the Gospels, Jesus seeks out people who need healing of soul. He reconciles sinners with God and their human community.
   ➤ Jesus will heal our souls, especially through two Sacraments: the Sacrament of Penance and Reconciliation and the Sacrament of Anointing of the Sick.

   But, we must desire healing, be sorry for our sins, and seek reconciliation with God, the Church, others, and ourselves. We must show that desire through prayer, the Eucharist, and acts that show our sorrow.

**14**

# Optional Activity

**Use** the chapter 14 activity handout, "Jesus Heals" (Document #: TX003523), to reinforce and assess the participants' understanding of Jesus' healing ministry and the Corporal and Spiritual Works of Mercy.

# Closing Prayer (5 minutes)

**Enlist** a couple volunteers to alternate reading the lines of the prayer in the Pray It! article on page 151 in the handbook. **Close** with the Sign of the Cross.

# Online Resources

To access activities and a quiz related to this chapter, go to *www.smp.org/resourcecenter/books/* and click on "Catechist: Additional Course Handouts or Quizzes." Tip sheets and links are also available.

# Jesus Heals

## Chapter 14 Summary

### Chapter Learning Objectives

- The participants will reflect on accounts of Jesus' spiritual and physical healing and how those accounts relate to their own lives.

- The participants will consider ways to bring Christ's healing to others.

### Content Summary

1. Miracles are special signs of God's power shown in Jesus and in human history. Miracles helped people to have faith in Jesus. In most cases, miracles relieved suffering and are signs of the love and compassion of the Kingdom.

2. Jesus healed people from a variety of social backgrounds.

3. Often Jesus tied his healing actions to faith in him.

4. Jesus often cured a person's body to improve that person's soul.

5. The main work of Jesus was to cure spiritual evils.

6. Jesus is a "doctor" who cures the illnesses that afflict our souls—pride, laziness, self-seeking, bad desires. Jesus wants us to find peace in him.

7. In the Gospels, Jesus seeks out people who need healing of soul. He reconciles sinners with God and their human community.

8. In the Gospels, Jesus also heals the souls of those who are close to him.

9. If we desire healing; are sorry for our sins; seek reconciliation with God, the Church, others, and ourselves; and show that desire through prayer, the Eucharist, and acts that show our sorrow, Jesus will heal our souls. He does this especially through two Sacraments: the Sacrament of Penance and Reconciliation and the Sacrament of Anointing of the Sick.

10. Jesus passes on to us the mission of healing, especially through the Works of Mercy.

11. The Corporal Works of Mercy concern the well-being of the body: for example, the need for food, drink, and clothing. The Spiritual Works of Mercy concern the well-being of the soul: for example, the need for advice, encouragement, and forgiveness.

12. When we do the Works of Mercy, we help to heal the wounds of those around us. Mostly we do this through our friendship, respect, concern, and prayer.

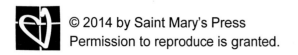

# Chapter 14 Activity: Jesus Heals

Match column A with column B to complete the sentences about Jesus' healing ministry.

**A**

1. Jesus sometimes used physical miracles

2. The Acts of the Apostles tell about the first Christians

3. The many miracles Jesus worked are

4. Most of Jesus' miracles relieved

5. Bartimaeus was

6. We can share in Jesus' healing mission by

7. Jesus passed on his mission to heal the body and soul

8. Zacchaeus was

**B**

___ a blind man whom Jesus cured.

___ healing in Jesus' name.

___ a tax collector who dishonestly collected extra money for himself, whose home Jesus visited.

___ to teach his followers about the life of the soul.

___ to his disciples.

___ people's suffering.

___ practicing the Works of Mercy.

___ special signs of God's presence and power in him.

## Sharing in Jesus' Healing Mission

Choose one Corporal Work of Mercy and one Spiritual Work of Mercy and give an example of how you can put each into practice.

**Corporal Work of Mercy:**

_____

**How I can live it:**

_____

_____

**Spiritual Work of Mercy:**

_____

**How I can live it:**

_____

_____

Document #: TX003523

# Chapter 15

# The Death of Jesus

## Preparation and Supplies

- Study chapter 15, "The Death of Jesus," in the handbook.
- Provide a Bible.
- Make copies of the chapter 15 activity handout, "Symbols of Jesus' Suffering" (Document #: TX003525), one for each pair.

## Pray It! (5 minutes)

**Tell** the participants that class will begin with a reading from Scripture that talks about what Jesus did for us. **Invite** a volunteer to read John 13:3–15. **Pray** the following:

> ➢ O giving God, we come before you today in a spirit of gratitude for all you have done for us. Amen.

**Close** with the Sign of the Cross.

## Study It! (40 to 50 minutes, depending on your class length)

### A. Jesus' Passion

1. **Ask** the young people to take out a sheet of paper and write a sentence or draw a picture in response to the following question: What did Jesus do for you? After everyone has had time to reflect and respond, **invite** a few volunteers to share their response to the question.

2. **Direct** the participants to read the chapter introduction and the section "Jesus' Passion," on pages 162–164 in the handbook. The content covers points 1 through 5 on the handout "Chapter 15 Summary" (Document #: TX003524).

3. *(Optional)* **Direct** the young people to the Think About It! article on page 164 in the handbook. **Ask** a volunteer to read the article aloud, and **use** the questions at the end to lead a discussion.

### B. Images of Jesus' Suffering and Death

1. **Direct** the participants to turn to pages 167 and 169 in the handbook. **Explain** the task as follows:

> ➢ Compare the two images of the Crucifixion in your handbook. These artistic interpretations of the Crucifixion use different styles to depict Jesus' death on the cross. A striking difference between them is the choice of colors and the use of light and darkness. Silently reflect on each of these images. On a sheet of paper, respond to the following questions:
> - What emotions does each image evoke?
> - Why are both styles a fitting way to depict Jesus' death on the cross? Provide specific details about each image to support your answer.
> - Which image more accurately reflects the way you understand and interpret the events of Jesus' suffering and death? Why?

When the young people have had enough time to reflect, **solicit** responses to the questions from volunteers.

2. **Direct** the participants to read the section "Images of Jesus' Suffering and Death," on pages 165–168 in the handbook. The content covers points 6 through 9 on the handout "Chapter 15 Summary" (Document #: TX003524).

3. *(Optional)* **Direct** the young people to read the "People of Faith" article on page 171 in the handbook. **Lead** a discussion on the following questions:

   ➢ Dismas was a criminal, sentenced to death for his misdeeds, yet he is honored by the Church as a saint. How can this give all followers of Jesus hope for forgiveness and mercy?

   ➢ How can Jesus' forgiveness of Dismas help you in how you treat others whom you see as sinful or immoral or who have hurt you by their actions?

## C. Jesus Frees Us from Death

**Direct** the participants to read the section "Jesus Frees Us from Death," on pages 168–170 in the handbook. The content covers point 10 on the handout "Chapter 15 Summary" (Document #: TX003524).

*Note:* If you are running short on time, you may wish to just briefly summarize this section.

## Live It! (10 to 15 minutes)

1. **Direct** the young people to form pairs. **Distribute** a copy of the chapter 15 activity handout, "Symbols of Jesus' Suffering"(Document #: TX003525), to each pair. **Explain** the task as follows:

   ➢ Each group is to decorate the cross shape on the handout with symbols that represent Jesus' suffering and death. Refer to the Stations of the Cross on page 165 in the handbook.

   ➢ Choose two of the symbols you have drawn and tell why you chose each symbol and what each expresses about Jesus' suffering and death.

2. **Invite** each pair to share what symbols they chose and why and to explain what each expresses about Jesus' suffering and death.

3. **Comment** as follows in your own words:

   ➢ Jesus' Passion and death teach us how much God loves us. From the Passion of Christ, we learn to bear our own sufferings with patience and to have compassion for the sufferings of others.

   ➢ The New Testament compares Christ in his suffering and death to several images that Jewish readers would recognize: the Passover Lamb, the Good Shepherd who gives his life for his sheep, the Suffering Servant from the Book of Isaiah.

   ➢ The suffering of Jesus reminds us that God, who loves us, brings good out of every evil.

**15**

## Closing Prayer (5 minutes)

**Direct** the participants to the Pray It! article on page 163 in the handbook. **Lead** the young people in praying the prayer together. **Close** with the Sign of the Cross.

## Online Resources

To access activities and a quiz related to this chapter, go to *www.smp.org/resourcecenter/books/* and click on "Catechist: Additional Course Handouts or Quizzes." Tip sheets and links are also available.

# The Death of Jesus

## Chapter 15 Summary

## Chapter Learning Objectives

- The participants will examine the events of Christ's Passion and death.

- The participants will understand that through his suffering and death, Jesus frees us from sin.

- The participants will reflect on the theme of sacrifice in their own lives.

## Content Summary

1. In Christ's Passion, his suffering and death on the cross, his saving work is completed. The Passion is Christ's final act of love for us.

2. In his suffering and death, Jesus gave himself freely for each of us.

3. During Holy Week and the Easter Season, we hear about Jesus' final sacrifice and about the victory of his Resurrection.

4. The events of Jesus' Passion are recorded in all four Gospels, but our handbook summarizes the account of the Gospel of Luke.

5. Jesus' Passion and death teach us how much God loves us. We learn both patience and compassion.

6. The New Testament compares Christ in his suffering and death to several images that Jewish readers would recognize: the Passover Lamb, the Good Shepherd, and the Suffering Servant.

7. The mystery of how Christ's Passion, death, Resurrection, and Ascension save us from sin and death is called the Paschal Mystery.

8. Suffering itself is a mystery. The suffering of Jesus reminds us that God, who loves us, brings good out of every evil.

9. If we unite our sufferings with the sufferings of Jesus, we can help Christ's saving action in the world.

10. Jesus accepted human death for our sake, so that we might know that death is not a final ending but a new beginning through his Resurrection.

# Chapter 15 Activity:
# Symbols of Jesus' Suffering

Decorate the cross shape below with symbols that represent Jesus' suffering and death. Refer to the Stations of the Cross on page 165 in the handbook. Choose two of the symbols you have drawn. Tell why you chose each symbol and what each one expresses about Jesus' suffering and death.

**Symbol:** _____

_____

_____

_____

_____

_____

**Symbol:** _____

_____

_____

_____

_____

_____

Document #: TX003525

# Chapter 16

# The Resurrection of Jesus

## Preparation and Supplies

- Study chapter 16, "The Resurrection of Jesus," in the handbook.
- Make copies of the chapter 16 activity handout, "Symbols of the Resurrection" (Document #: TX003527), one for each participant.
- Provide a Bible, three sheets of newsprint, and a set of markers for each group.

## Pray It! (5 minutes)

**Tell** the participants that class will begin with a reading from Scripture that recalls one of Jesus' appearances to his disciples after his Resurrection. **Invite** a volunteer to read John 20:19–20. **Pray** the following:

> ➢ Lord of hope, when we are feeling hopeless or discouraged, help us to remember the joyful promise of your Resurrection. May our faith be strong and our trust in you complete! Amen.

**Close** with the Sign of the Cross.

## Study It! (35 to 45 minutes, depending on your class length)

### A. The Risen Christ

1. **Distribute** a copy of the chapter 16 activity handout, "Symbols of the Resurrection" (Document #: TX003527), to each young person. **Direct** the participants to complete the first activity, either alone or in pairs. **Encourage** them to be creative in choosing symbols from nature to represent the hope of the Resurrection. When everyone has finished, **ask** volunteers to share their drawings and explanations.

2. **Direct** the young people to read the chapter introduction and the section "The Risen Christ," on pages 172–176 in the handbook. The content covers points 1 through 4 on the handout "Chapter 16 Summary" (Document #: TX003526).

3. *(Optional)* **Direct** the participants to the Think About It! article on page 175 in the handbook. **Invite** a volunteer to read the article aloud, and **use** the questions at the end to lead a discussion.

### B. The Ascension

1. **Direct** the young people to the second half of the chapter 16 activity handout, "Symbols of the Resurrection" (Document #: TX003527). **Ask** the participants, either alone or in pairs, to complete the Easter acrostic with a word or phrase that begins with each letter, making sure that the words or phrases are especially meaningful and creative. **Write** the word *EASTER* on the board vertically. **Ask** volunteers to share the words and phrases they came up with for each letter. **Record** their responses on the board next to the appropriate letter.

2. **Direct** the young people to read the section "The Ascension," on pages 176–180 in the handbook. The content covers points 5 through 10 on the handout "Chapter 16 Summary" (Document #: TX003526).

**16**

3. *(Optional)* **Direct** the participants to the Liturgy Connection article on page 176 in the handbook. **Invite** a volunteer to read the article aloud, and **lead** a discussion of why funerals, although sad events, can also be occasions of hope. **Lead** the discussion to the message that because of Jesus' own Resurrection, our own death does not mean an end to life but the beginning of a new life with God in Heaven.

## Live It! (15 to 20 minutes)

1. **Organize** the young people into groups of three or four. **Distribute** a Bible, three sheets of newsprint, and a set of markers to each group. **Explain** the task as follows:
   - ➤ Each group is to read the account of Jesus' Ascension in the Acts of the Apostles 1:6–11.
   - ➤ On the three sheets of newsprint, design a triptych that shows three images related to the Ascension. *(Explain that a triptych is a work of art divided into three sections, often hinged together, showing images related to a central theme. The middle panel is usually larger than the other two and is the central focus of the triptych.)*
   - ➤ On the bottom of each panel, write one way that young people today can witness to and participate in Christ's kingly mission.
2. When everyone has finished, **display** the artwork around the room. **Invite** volunteers to share and explain their illustrations and what they wrote.
3. **Comment** as follows in your own words:
   - ➤ For forty days after his Resurrection, Jesus completes his teaching. He gives his Apostles and disciples instructions. On the fortieth day after Easter, he returns to his Father. This return is called the Ascension into Heaven.
   - ➤ In Jesus, humanity enters Heaven. Jesus sits at God's right hand—the symbol of power—and fully shares in the power of God.
   - ➤ As followers of Jesus, we continue his mission of announcing his Kingdom of love and helping to hasten its coming upon earth.
   - ➤ Before his return to Heaven, Jesus promised to send the Holy Spirit to us to guide and strengthen us.

## Closing Prayer (5 minutes)

**Direct** the participants to the Pray It! article on page 173 in the handbook. **Invite** a volunteer to read the prayer aloud. **Ask** the young people to silently think of ways they can continue Jesus' mission of love in their own lives. **Conclude** with the following:
   - ➤ Jesus, our Divine Companion, may we come closer to you in friendship and, in so doing, become closer to one another. Amen.

**Close** with the Sign of the Cross.

## Online Resources

To access activities and a quiz related to this chapter, go to *www.smp.org/resourcecenter/books/* and click on "Catechist: Additional Course Handouts or Quizzes." Tip sheets and links are also available.

**16**

# The Resurrection of Jesus

## Chapter 16 Summary

### Chapter Learning Objectives

- The participants will explore the events surrounding Jesus' Resurrection.

- The participants will examine ways the Resurrection is a source of hope for all people.

- The participants will reflect on Jesus' Ascension and how they can witness to and participate in Jesus' kingly mission in their own lives.

### Content Summary

1. The Resurrection of Jesus on the Sunday after Good Friday is a key fact of our faith. It is God's greatest miracle and enables us to understand our faith and to live it rightly.

2. The disciples of Jesus did not expect Jesus to die such a horrible death; neither did they expect Jesus to rise victoriously from the dead. Only after they had seen Jesus with their own eyes did they believe such an amazing reality.

3. In his Resurrection, the body and soul of Jesus are reunited. His body is still human, showing the scars of his suffering and death. But it is now glorified with divine life.

4. We begin to share in the death and Resurrection of Jesus when we are baptized. We are united with God and become his children, the brothers and sisters of his Son, Jesus Christ. In and through Jesus, we too will be resurrected.

5. For forty days after his Resurrection, Jesus completes his teaching. He gives his Apostles and disciples instructions. Then, on the fortieth day after Easter, he returns to his Father. This return is called the Ascension into Heaven.

6. In Jesus, humanity enters Heaven. Jesus sits at God's right hand—the symbol of power—and fully shares in the power of God.

7. As followers of Jesus, we continue his mission of announcing his Kingdom of love and helping to hasten its coming upon earth.

8. Before his return to Heaven, Jesus promised to send the Holy Spirit to us to guide and strengthen us.

9. Jesus will come again in glory at the end of time to reveal himself to the entire world. At this time, at the Last Judgment, Jesus will judge the living and the dead. Knowing each person, Jesus will judge each of us fairly.

10. Jesus will come first of all to save us, to bring us with him into God's Kingdom—as long as we do not reject him. This is a decision we make each day, as we keep trying to grow in the Spirit, in love and compassion.

(All summary points are taken from *The Catholic Connections Handbook for Middle Schoolers, Second Edition.* Copyright © 2014 by Saint Mary's Press. All rights reserved.)

# Chapter 16 Activity:
# Symbols of the Resurrection

One of the symbols the Church uses to represent Christ's Resurrection is the lily. This beautiful white flower comes to life in the spring, reborn from a lifeless bulb. It resembles a trumpet, an instrument used to announce important news, especially victory. What other symbols from nature might represent Jesus' Resurrection? In the space below, draw an image of something from nature that symbolizes the Resurrection. Then explain your illustration.

_____

_____

## Easter Acrostic

Christians celebrate Jesus' Resurrection on Easter. In the following acrostic, write a word or phrase related to the Resurrection that begins with each letter. One has been done for you.

E *ternal life* _____

A _____

S _____

T _____

E _____

R _____

Document #: TX003527

# Chapter 17

# The Holy Spirit

## Preparation and Supplies

- Study chapter 17, "The Holy Spirit," in the handbook.
- Provide a Bible.
- Provide sheets of white stationery paper, envelopes, and sheets of blank paper, one of each for each participant. *(optional)*
- Gather a sheet of newsprint and a marker for each pair.
- Make copies of the chapter 17 activity handout, "Spirit News Activity" (Document #: TX003529), one for each pair.

## Pray It! (5 minutes)

**Tell** the participants that class will begin with a prayer to the Holy Spirit. **Invite** a volunteer to read Galatians 5:22–25. **Direct** the young people to turn to the Pray It! article on page 183 in the handbook. **Lead** them in praying the prayer together. **Close** with the Sign of the Cross.

## Study It! (35 to 45 minutes, depending on your class length)

### A. The Breath of God

1. **Direct** the participants to form pairs. **Explain** the task as follows:
   ➢ Each of you will time your partner to see how many normal breaths you each can take in 1 minute. A full breath includes both an inhale and an exhale. Keep a tally for each other.

   After a few minutes, **give** the following instructions:
   ➢ Now see if you each can hold your breath for 30 seconds—no cheating allowed—when I say "Go."

   After a minute, **ask** the young people to describe what it feels like to keep holding their breath while their brain is screaming, "Breathe! Breathe!"

2. **Direct** the participants to read the chapter introduction and the section "The Breath of God," on pages 182–184 in the handbook. The content covers points 1 through 3 on the handout "Chapter 17 Summary" (Document #: TX003528).

3. *(Optional)* **Direct** the young people to the Live It! article on page 190 in the handbook. **Ask** a volunteer to read the article aloud. **Invite** the participants to think of persons who truly live God's love, who "breathe out" God's love upon others. **Distribute** a sheet of stationery paper and an envelope to each young person. Give them a few minutes to write a thank-you note to one person who came to mind. *(You may want to distribute blank paper also, to use as practice paper.)* As needed, review the conventions of letter-writing (date, "Dear," and complimentary close). Strategize ways to deliver or mail the notes.

### B. God's Spirit Prepares the Way

1. **Write** the word *breath* on the board. With the entire group, **brainstorm** other words or ideas about breath. **Write** down each word or idea suggested. Considering all the words and ideas, **find** descriptive words and images that can be linked to the Holy Spirit. If ideas are negative ("not breathing" or "suffocating"), **link** those words to the experience of living without the Holy Spirit.

2. **Direct** the participants to read the sections "The Holy Spirit Prepares the Way," "In the Fullness of Time," and "Jesus and the Holy Spirit," on pages 185–188 in the handbook. The content covers points 4 through 6 on the handout "Chapter 17 Summary" (Document #: TX003528).

3. *(Optional)* **Direct** the young people to the Liturgy Connection article on page 187 in the handbook. **Invite** a volunteer to read the article aloud. **Lead** a discussion on the following question: What does the Holy Spirit do at this moment in the Eucharistic Prayer? *(The Spirit makes these gifts holy so that they can become the Body and Blood of Christ.)* **Remind** the participants to listen for these words the next time they participate in the Mass.

## C. On a Mission

**Direct** the participants to read the section "On a Mission," on pages 189–190 in the handbook. The content covers points 7 through 9 on the handout "Chapter 17 Summary" (Document #: TX003528).

*Note:* If you are running short on time, you may wish to just briefly summarize this section.

## Live It! (15 to 20 minutes)

1. **Arrange** the young people in pairs. **Give** each pair a sheet of newsprint, a marker, and a copy of the chapter 17 activity handout, "Spirit News Activity" (Document #: TX003529). **Explain** the task as follows:

   ➢ You and your partner are going to be reporting on the Holy Spirit's activity in the world. Please follow along on the handout as I read through the steps for the activity.

   After reading the instructions, **check** for understanding by asking a few of the participants to repeat back their understanding of what they are going to do in their pairs.

2. **Invite** each pair to present its headlines to the large group. **Post** the newsprint sheets around the room.

3. **Comment** as follows in your own words:

   ➢ The Holy Spirit continues to act in the world and in the Church today, bringing people to Christ. The Holy Spirit helps us to understand Jesus' death and Resurrection, and makes the mystery of Christ present in the Eucharist and in the other Sacraments. The Holy Spirit works in the Church to build her up, to bring her life, and to make her holy.

   ➢ Another name for the Holy Spirit, found in the Gospel of John, is Advocate, or helper and supporter. An advocate is someone who "speaks for" someone else. The Holy Spirit is always with us, is always at our side and on our side.

## Closing Prayer (5 minutes)

**Ask** the participants to reflect silently for a minute in gratitude for the presence of God's Spirit in the Church and the world. **Direct** the young people to find the "Prayer to the Holy Spirit" on page 560 in the handbook. **Lead** them in praying together. **Close** with the Sign of the Cross.

## Online Resources

To access activities and a quiz related to this chapter, go to *www.smp.org/resourcecenter/books/* and click on "Catechist: Additional Course Handouts or Quizzes." Tip sheets and links are also available.

# The Holy Spirit

## Chapter 17 Summary

### Chapter Learning Objectives

- The participants will explore the meaning of the Holy Spirit as the Breath of God.

- The participants will name concrete ways they see the Holy Spirit present in the world.

### Content Summary

1. The Holy Spirit is the Third Divine Person of the Blessed Trinity.

2. The Father, the Son, and the Holy Spirit are one God, united and inseparable.

3. The Holy Spirit is called the Breath of God, breathing God's life and love into us.

4. We learn about the Holy Spirit throughout Sacred Scripture, beginning with the Book of Genesis. Throughout the Old Testament, the Spirit of God works quietly, behind the scenes, to prepare God's people for the Messiah.

5. In the New Testament, the Holy Spirit prepared Mary to become the Mother of God. In the Gospel of Luke, Jesus announced his mission by proclaiming that the Holy Spirit was upon him to bring salvation to God's people.

6. In the Gospel of John, the newly risen Jesus visits his disciples and breathes the Holy Spirit upon them, the Spirit of peace, love, and forgiveness.

7. On Pentecost, the Holy Spirit comes upon the disciples with the power of wind and fire, giving them courage to preach the message of Jesus to the world.

8. The Holy Spirit continues to act in the Church today, bringing people to Christ. The Holy Spirit helps us to understand Jesus' death and Resurrection and makes the mystery of Christ present in the Eucharist and in the other Sacraments. The Holy Spirit works in the Church to build her up, to bring her life, and to make her holy.

9. Another name for the Holy Spirit, found in the Gospel of John, is Advocate, or helper and supporter. An advocate is someone who "speaks for" someone else. The Holy Spirit is always with us, always at our side and on our side.

# Chapter 17 Activity: Spirit News Activity

The editor of the *Spirit News,* a newspaper whose goal is to report how the Holy Spirit is active in the world, has asked for story ideas about ways the Holy Spirit is at work in the world. You and your partner have been asked to do the following:

1. Brainstorm ways you have seen the Holy Spirit active in the lives of others or in your own lives.

2. After you have both had an opportunity to share, decide on three stories that the two of you feel are worthy of being covered in the *Spirit News.* These stories should be actual examples of how you have seen the Holy Spirit at work in the lives of others or in your own lives.

3. You and your partner will then come up with three headlines that describe the Spirit success stories. Each headline can have a subhead that further describes the story in one or two sentences.

4. Your next task is to prepare a presentation about each of the three headlines that will convince the editor that the stories are worthy of publication.

5. One of you will present to the large group your headlines and the reasons these stories need to be told.

# Spirit News

Document #: TX003529

# Chapter 18

# Grace and the Gifts of the Holy Spirit

Preparation and Supplies

- Study chapter 18, "Grace and the Gifts of the Holy Spirit," in the handbook.
- Write "God's grace" on an index card and insert the card into a box with a lid. Wrap the box with wrapping paper, and display prominently.
- Make copies of the chapter 18 activity handout, "Symbols of the Gifts of the Holy Spirit" (Document #: TX003531), one for each pair.

## Pray It! (5 minutes)

**Tell** the participants that class will begin with a prayer asking for God's grace. **Ask** a couple volunteers to take turns reading John 14:15–26. **Direct** the young people to the Pray It! article on page 193 in the handbook. **Lead** them in praying the prayer together. **Close** with the Sign of the Cross.

## Study It! (40 to 50 minutes, depending on your class length)

### A. God Takes the First Step

1. **Direct** the participants' attention to the gift-wrapped box at the front of the room. **Lead** a discussion by asking the following questions:

   ➢ If this could be any gift in the world, just for you, what would you want it to be?
   ➢ If inside this box is the best gift in the world that you could give to somebody else, what would it be?

   After volunteers have an opportunity to share their responses, **ask** the young people what they think God would put in the box. Listen to their responses. **Invite** someone to come forward and remove the card from the box. **Ask** him or her to read the card aloud: "God's grace." **Write** the phrase on the board. **Invite** volunteers to think about and then offer words and phrases that define or describe God's grace. **Create** a mind map by writing their responses around the phrase and connecting them to the main phrase by drawing lines.

2. **Direct** the participants to read the chapter introduction and the section "God Takes the First Step," on pages 192–194 in the handbook. The content covers points 1 through 3 on the handout "Chapter 18 Summary" (Document #: TX003530).

3. *(Optional)* **Direct** the young people to the Live It! article on page 200 in the handbook. **Read** the article aloud. **Ask** the participants to share examples of evidence of God's grace they may have seen today.

### B. Let God's Grace In

1. **Direct** the young people to the Think About It! article on page 194 in the handbook. **Invite** them to reflect on the question at the end of the article. **Ask** volunteers to share their responses. You may want to start by offering a response of your own.

**18**

2. **Direct** the participants to read the sections "Let God's Grace In," "Give Love Away," and "Everything Is Possible with God's Grace," on pages 194–198 in the handbook. The content covers points 4 through 6 on the handout "Chapter 18 Handout" (Document #: TX003530).

3. *(Optional)* **Direct** the young people to locate the job description for being a Christian on page 196 in the handbook. For each of the job responsibilities, **ask** a volunteer to name a way he or she could fulfill that responsibility. If necessary, **refer** to the ideas listed on page 198 in the handbook, in the second paragraph under the heading "Everything Is Possible with God's Grace."

## C. The Gifts of the Holy Spirit

**Direct** the participants to read the section "The Gifts of the Holy Spirit," on pages 198–201 in the handbook. The content covers points 7 through 9 on the handout "Chapter 18 Summary" (Document #: TX003530).

*Note:* If you are running short on time, you may wish to just briefly summarize this section.

## Live It! (10 to 15 minutes)

1. **Direct** the young people to find a partner. **Distribute** the chapter 18 activity handout, "Symbols of the Gifts of the Holy Spirit" (Document #: TX003531), to each pair. **Explain** the task as follows:
    ➢ You and your partner are to complete the names of the Gifts of the Holy Spirit on the handout. You can refer to pages 198–201 in the handbook.
    ➢ After reading the description of each of the gifts, draw a suitable symbol for each.

2. **Invite** volunteers from each group to share and explain the symbols they drew for each gift.

3. **Comment** as follows in your own words:
    ➢ The Gifts of the Holy Spirit are seven graces that help us respond to God's call to love others and to live holy lives.
    ➢ The Gifts of the Holy Spirit are Wisdom, Understanding, Right Judgment (Counsel), Courage (Fortitude), Knowledge, Reverence (Piety), and Wonder and Awe (Fear of the Lord).
    ➢ In Confirmation, the Gifts of the Holy Spirit are strengthened in us. They help us to live lives of faith and to love as fully initiated members of the Church.

## Closing Prayer (5 minutes)

**Direct** the participants to the Liturgy Connection article on page 198. **Read** the explanation in the article. **Ask** the young people to silently reflect on which Gift of the Holy Spirit they are in need of during this time in their lives. After a moment of silence, **pray** the prayer the Bishop prays at Confirmation. **Close** with the Sign of the Cross.

## Online Resources

To access activities and a quiz related to this chapter, go to *www.smp.org/resourcecenter/books/* and click on "Catechist: Additional Course Handouts or Quizzes." Tip sheets and links are also available.

**18**

# Grace and the Gifts of the Holy Spirit

## Chapter 18 Summary

### Chapter Learning Objectives

- The participants will explore the gift of God's grace.

- The participants will examine the responsibilities of being a Christian and how the Gifts of the Holy Spirit help us to participate in God's life.

### Content Summary

1. Grace is the gift of God's loving presence in our lives, the help he gives through the Holy Spirit to participate in divine life.

2. At Baptism we receive the life and love of the Holy Spirit. This gift of grace draws us into a close relationship with the Father and Jesus Christ and makes us God's adopted sons and daughters.

3. Only God can fully satisfy the longings of the human heart. Through grace, we have the ability to freely know and love God. Because God loves us no matter what, he does not force us to love him in return.

4. A person who says yes to God's invitation to participate in his life acts in a way that reflects the values of Jesus. We do good works out of love for God. All our good works are the result of God's grace working in us.

5. When we choose to give love away, as God does, we open ourselves more and more to the gifts of love and grace God constantly offers us. Like Jesus, we can be in-the-flesh grace for others.

6. People who accept the gift of God's grace open that gift and use it in their everyday lives. They grow in their Catholic faith, and they love God and neighbor.

7. The Gifts of the Holy Spirit are seven graces that help us respond to God's call to love others and to live holy lives.

8. The Gifts of the Holy Spirit are Wisdom, Understanding, Right Judgment (Counsel), Courage (Fortitude), Knowledge, Reverence (Piety), and Wonder and Awe (Fear of the Lord).

9. In Confirmation, the Gifts of the Holy Spirit are strengthened in us. They help us to live lives of faith and love as fully initiated members of the Church.

# Chapter 18 Activity:
# Symbols of the Gifts of the Holy Spirit

The Gifts of the Holy Spirit help us to love God. Each gives us special graces to respond to God's call to live holy lives. Complete the names of the Gifts of the Holy Spirit, and draw a suitable symbol for each.

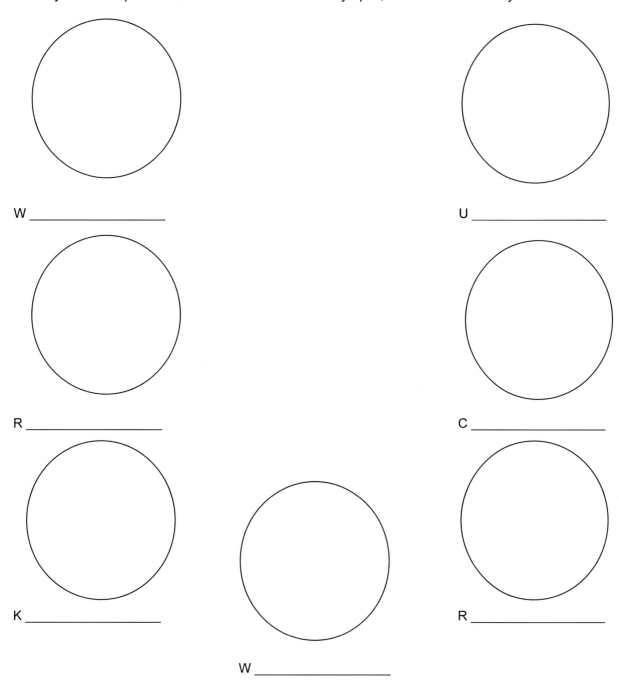

W _____

U _____

R _____

C _____

K _____

W _____

R _____

Document #: TX003531

# Life Issues A

## Who Am I?

### Preparation and Supplies

- Provide a Bible, one for each group.
- Make copies of the life issues A activity handout, "I Am God's Gift to the World" (Document #: TX003533), one for each participant.
- Provide ribbons, 10 inches in length, one for each participant.
- Set a basket on a table in the front of the room.

### Pray It! (5 minutes)

**Tell** the participants that in this lesson we are going to be examining who we are and who God made us to be. **Invite** a volunteer to read Genesis 1:26–28. **Pray** the following:

> ➤ God our Father, you created each of us in your image, yet we are all different. Give us the courage to be ourselves, to be the unique persons you created us to be. Remind us that when we respect one another's differences, we also respect you, because it is you who made each of us to be who we are. Amen.

**Close** with the Sign of the Cross.

### Study It! (40 to 50 minutes, depending on your class length)

#### A. Who Are We?

1. **Ask** the young people to share stereotypes they have observed or experienced. Though some stereotypes are pretty standard (those about athletes, for example), many evolve and change over time. Feel free to **include** reflections on the memories of cliques and stereotypes from your own youth.

2. **Comment** as follows in your own words:
   > ➤ Many times we identify ourselves by what we like—for example, by our favorite music, sports, or hobbies.
   > ➤ Sometimes we are identified by the groups we belong to. You might be a citizen of the United States, or you might go to *(insert name of local school)*. You belong to a certain race. You are Catholic.
   > ➤ Being identified with a group is fine. It is good to be a part of a larger community. In fact, much of our faith is about being part of something larger than ourselves.
   > ➤ Nonetheless we are more than what we like, where we live, the school we attend, or the race we are.
   > ➤ To find out who we truly are, we can turn to God. God speaks to us through the Church, through the Bible, and through prayer.

3. *(Optional).* **Direct** the participants to the Live It! article on page 86 in chapter 7, "The Human Person," in the handbook. **Ask** a volunteer to read the article aloud. **Brainstorm** with the young people ways they can respond kindly to others, especially those who insult or hurt them.

#### B. Who We Are according to God

1. **Organize** the large group into groups of three or four. **Distribute** a Bible to each group, and **assign** each group one of the following Scripture passages:
   - Genesis 2:18
   - Matthew 5:14–16
   - Luke 12:22–27

- 1 Corinthians 6:18–20
- 1 Corinthians 12:12–20,27
- Ephesians 5:1–2
- Colossians 2:12–14

**Explain** the task as follows:

➢ Each group has 5 minutes to read the passage listed and to discuss as follows:
  - What does this passage say about human beings?
  - What does it say about how we should act toward one another or to God's creation?

After time is up, **invite** each group to read its passage and share its responses with the large group. **Lead** a short discussion to summarize the responses.

2. **Comment** as follows in your own words:

➢ Human beings are good. There is nothing we or anyone else can do to take this goodness away.

➢ Though we are always good, we do not always do good things. There is a difference between being good and doing good things.

➢ God made each of us differently. Each of us has a particular role that no one else can accomplish. Some of us have gifts and talents that others do not. Our job is to share our gifts and talents with one another.

➢ Every human being is a creature of God and is therefore loved by God, regardless of nationality, race, gender, or religion.

3. *(Optional)* **Direct** the participants to the Did You Know? article on page 81 in chapter 7, "The Human Person," in the handbook. **Invite** a volunteer to read the article aloud. **Lead** a discussion on ways the Church cares about all aspects of human life.

## Live It! (10 to 15 minutes)

1. **Distribute** to each young person a copy of the life issues A activity handout, "I Am God's Gift to the World" (Document #: TX003533), and a ribbon. **Direct** the participants to spread out around the room and to quietly complete the handout.

2. When everyone has finished, **give** the following instructions:

➢ Each of you is to roll your handout up and tie it with the ribbon I gave you.

➢ Then bring your handout up and place it in the basket as an offering to God and to one another.

3. When everyone has finished, **comment** as follows:

➢ This activity teaches us that each and every life is a gift. Your life is not only God's gift to you; it is God's gift to everyone else. Your gift and responsibility is to develop the gifts and talents God gave you. Placing the scroll that describes who you are in the basket is a sign of your offering the gift of yourself to God and to one another.

## Closing Prayer (5 minutes)

**Ask** a volunteer to read Psalm 139:1–16 aloud. **Pray** the following:

➢ Lord, we offer up the most special gift we have to give: ourselves. You gave us the gift of life. In return, we pledge to live our lives in a way that pleases you. Amen.

**Close** with the Sign of the Cross.

## Online Resources

To access activities and a quiz related to this chapter, go to *www.smp.org/resourcecenter/books/* and click on "Catechist: Additional Course Handouts or Quizzes." Tip sheets and links are also available.

# Who Am I?

## Life Issues A Summary

### Chapter Learning Objectives

- The participants will be helped to appreciate their unique selves as gifts of God.

- The participants will be encouraged to see themselves created by God as basically good.

- The participants will be encouraged to take responsibility for developing their gifts and talents to the best of their ability.

### Content Summary

1. Being identified with a group is fine. It is good to be a part of a larger community. In fact, much of our faith is about being part of something larger than ourselves.

2. Nonetheless we are more than what we like, where we live, the school we attend, or the race we are.

3. To find out who we truly are, we can turn to God. God speaks to us through the Church, through the Bible, and through prayer.

4. Human beings are good. There is nothing we or anyone else can do to take this goodness away.

5. Though we are always good, we do not always do good things. There is a difference between being good and doing good things.

6. God made each of us differently. Each of us has a particular role that no one else can accomplish. Some of us have gifts and talents that others do not. Our job is to share our gifts and talents with one another.

7. Every human being is a creature of God and is therefore loved by God, regardless of nationality, race, gender, or religion.

8. All of our lives are gifts. Your life is not just God's gift to you; it is God's gift to everyone else.

9. Your gift and responsibility is to develop the gifts and talents God gave you to the best of your ability.

Document #: TX003532

# Life Issues A Activity:
# I Am God's Gift to the World

I am _____ *(your name)*. I am made in the image of God, not because of what I can do or what I look like, but simply because I am his child. God has given me a light to shine by giving me the gifts of _____ *(list two or three of your gifts and talents)*. During this life I will have many roles. I may not always know what my role is, but right now I know that I am_____ *(list a few important roles you have: son, sister, friend, student, granddaughter, volunteer, tutor, Girl Scout, Boy Scout, team captain, and so on)*.

But I cannot do everything on my own. God has also placed _____ _____ *(list your family members)* in my life. They are people I love and who love me by _____ *(list what your parents and other family members do for you)*. I am a member of the communities of _____ *(name your church)* and _____ *(name your school)*.

I am a temple of the Holy Spirit to whom God has given the qualities of _____ _____ *(joy, honesty, courageousness, curiosity, loyalty, humor, and so on)*.

I am not God's gift to myself. I was not placed here to seek my own pleasure, but to serve. I serve others by _____ *(list a few good things you do for others)*.

I am God's unique gift to the world. I am _____ *(your name)*.

Document #: TX003533

# Life Issues B
## Friends in Jesus

### Preparation and Supplies

- Provide two to four Bibles.
- Gather a sheet of newsprint and a set of markers for each of four groups.
- Make copies of the life issues B activity handout, "WWYD (What Would You Do?) Role-Playing Scenarios" (Document #: TX003535), cut apart, one for each group.

### Pray It! (5 minutes)

**Tell** the participants that in this lesson we are going to be exploring friendship and how Jesus is a role model for being a good friend. **Invite** a volunteer to read John 15:15. **Pray** the following:

> ➤ Lord, help us to imitate you as we share in the joys and struggles of friendship with one another. We thank you for your faithful friendship! Amen.

**Close** with the Sign of the Cross.

### Study It! (40 to 50 minutes, depending on your class length)

#### A. Friend or Foe?

1. **Organize** the young people into four groups. **Distribute** a sheet of newsprint and a set of markers to each group. **Assign** one of the following names to each group, to be written at the top of the sheet: Friendly Francine, Caring Carl, Mean Maggie, and Bullying Billy. **Explain** the task as follows:
   - ➤ Each group is to create a cartoon character that will help us to explore "being a friend." The character will have either good or not-so-good friendship skills.
   - ➤ The groups drawing Friendly Francine and Caring Carl will draw characters with positive traits of friendship. For example, Friendly Francine: big ears because she is a good listener. Caring Carl: a strong back to carry his friends when they are hurting.
   - ➤ The groups drawing Mean Maggie and Bullying Billy will draw characters with negative traits. For example, Mean Maggie might have a forked tongue because she tells lies about others. Bullying Billy might have big hands because he is always pushing people around.
   - ➤ Group members will add as many positive or negative traits of friendship to their drawings as they can. They will identify those characteristics by writing a description of each and pointing to that part of the drawing with an arrow.
2. When the groups have finished, **invite** each to present its drawing to the large group. **Lead** a discussion about friendship based on the drawings.
3. *(Optional)* **Use** the following questions to extend the discussion:
   - ➤ When we think about being a good friend, we don't think about confrontation.
   - ➤ Can it sometimes be good to confront our friends? In what situations?
   - ➤ When does confrontation "cross the line" and become hurtful?

#### B. Jesus: A Model Friend

1. **Organize** the large group into either two or four groups. **Distribute** a Bible to each group. **Assign** each group one of the following Scripture passages: (A) Matthew 14:22–23, Jesus Walks on the Water, or (B) Matthew 26:36–46, Jesus Prays in Gethsemane. **Explain the** task as follows:
   - ➤ Each group has 5 minutes to read its passage. How does Jesus act as a friend?

2. **Invite** each group to read its passage and to share the ways Jesus acts as a good friend. **Comment** as follows in your own words:

> (A) Good friends take time away by themselves for prayer and reflection. (Jesus goes to the mountain alone to pray.)

> (A) Good friends encourage each other. (Jesus encourages the disciples not to be afraid in the storm.)

> (A) Good friends invite each other to be positive risk takers. (Jesus invites Peter to walk on the water toward him.)

> (A) Friends reach out to help each other when they are in trouble, even if they don't approve of the friend's behavior. (Jesus reaches out immediately to help Peter, but rebukes him for lack of faith.)

> (B) Good friends gather with a few close friends in troubled times. (Jesus walks off to pray with Peter, John, and James.)

> (B) Good friends share their thoughts openly. (Jesus shares that his heart is deeply troubled.)

> (B) Good friends ask for support in time of need. (Jesus asks the three to keep watch.)

> (B) Good friends express their concerns when friends let them down. (Jesus rebukes Peter, John, and James for falling asleep.)

> (B) Good friends choose to sometimes "let it go." (Jesus says nothing when he finds the disciples asleep for the second time.)

> (B) Good friends give each other "wake-up calls" when needed. (Jesus wakes the disciples and warns them that the betrayer is near.)

3. *(Optional)* **Direct** the participants to the Live It! article on page 123 in chapter 11, "Jesus Christ, True God and True Man," in the handbook. **Use** the article to lead a discussion on ways to know Jesus better.

# Live It! (10 to 15 minutes)

1. **Organize** the participants into groups of two or four, depending on the assigned scenario. **Distribute** a section of the life issues B activity handout, "WWYD (What Would You Do?) Role-Playing Scenarios" (Document #: TX003535), to each group. **Explain** the task as follows:

> Each group is to explore the question "What would you do?" in the assigned role-play scenario and then apply Jesus' example of friendship to the scenario. Discuss as a group how you will role-play this scene for the large group.

2. **Invite** each small group to role-play its scenario in front of the large group.

3. After each presentation, **lead** the young people in applying Jesus' example to each scene.

# Closing Prayer (5 minutes)

**Conclude** with the following:

> Jesus, our Divine Companion, may we come closer to you in friendship and, in so doing, become closer to one another. Amen.

**Close** with the Sign of the Cross.

# Online Resources

To access activities and a quiz related to this chapter, go to *www.smp.org/resourcecenter/books/* and click on "Catechist: Additional Course Handouts or Quizzes." Tip sheets and links are also available.

Life
Issues B

# Friends in Jesus

## Life Issues B Summary

### Chapter Learning Objectives

- The participants will be helped to appreciate the qualities of a good friend.

- The participants will be encouraged to appreciate Jesus as a model friend.

- The participants will be encouraged to imitate Jesus in applying his values and attitudes of friendship and love to their own relationships with others.

### Content Summary

1. In experiences of meeting other people, we have some sense of what it means to be a good friend.

2. We can look to Jesus as our model of friendship, particularly in two accounts: Matthew 14:22–23 (Jesus Walks on the Water) and Matthew 26:36–46 (Jesus Prays in Gethsemane).

3. From the account of Jesus' walking on the water, we learn that (1) good friends take time away by themselves for prayer and reflection, (2) good friends encourage each other, (3) good friends invite each other to be positive risk takers, and (4) good friends reach out to help each other.

4. From the account of Jesus in the garden at Gethsemane, we learn that (1) good friends gather with a few close friends in troubled times, (2) good friends share their thoughts openly, (3) good friends ask for support in time of need, (4) good friends express their concerns when friends let them down, (5) good friends sometimes choose to "let it go", and (6) good friends give each other wake-up calls.

5. In our relationships with others, we see Jesus as our model of friendship, and try to think and act with his attitudes and values.

# Life Issues B Activity: WWYD (What Would You Do?) Role-Playing Scenarios

Gabe is feeling stressed and overwhelmed. He decides he needs some time to think and pray. Just as he begins, three of his friends burst into his room and try to get him to play video games instead.

Veronica is on the diving team. She has never done a double flip before. She is standing on the edge of the board, trying to work up the nerve to attempt the dive. Her friend Nyesha is standing on the deck below her.

Manuel is upset with Austin. The two of them have been working on a group science project for the last two weeks. Austin did very little work on the project and as a result the group grade was a D. Later that day, after receiving the grade, Manuel sees Austin in the hallway.

Miranda got in big trouble and was suspended from school for two days for spray-painting "Miranda loves Bobby" on the school wall. She is upset about the suspension. On her way home from school that day, she runs into her friend Blake.

Joseph has been friends with Sanjeev since they were in kindergarten. Lately Sanjeev has been hanging out with some kids who Joseph feels will be a bad influence on Sanjeev. Joseph goes over to Sanjeev's house to talk to him.

Document #: TX003535

# Answer Keys

## Answer Key for Chapter 2 Activity

Sequence:

7 2 5 9 3 10 4 6 1 8

## Answer Key for Chapter 3 Activity

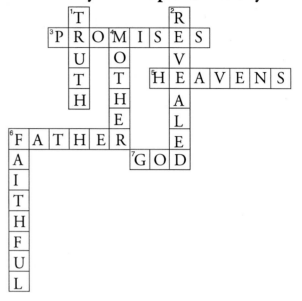

## Answer Key for Chapter 4 Activity

### A Prayer to the Trinity

Cryptogram solution:
In the name of the Father, and of the Son, and of the Holy Spirit.

## Answer Key for Chapter 7 Activity

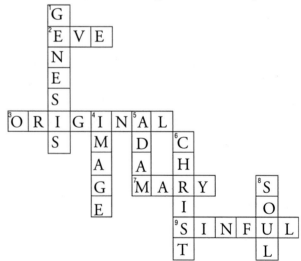

## Answer Key for Chapter 8 Activity

3. Go to Mass on Sunday and on Holy Days of Obligation.

4. We must obey our parents and treat them with respect.

7. Do not take what does not belong to you.

8. Do not lie or deceive others in any way.

10. We must not envy others' material wealth or possessions.

## Answer Key for Chapter 12 Activity

1. Mary
2. the Magi, or the Wise Men
3. Mary and Joseph
4. Mary
5. Jesus
6. Saint Nicholas of Myra
7. the Holy Spirit
8. the angel Gabriel
9. King Herod
10. Jesus

## Answer Key for Chapter 14 Activity

**Jesus Heals**

Answers for column B:

5 a blind man whom Jesus cured.

2 healing in Jesus' name.

8 a tax collector who dishonestly collected extra money for himself, whose home Jesus visited.

1 to teach his followers about the life of the soul.

7 to his disciples.

4 people's suffering.

6 practicing the Works of Mercy.

3 special signs of God's presence and power in him.

## Answer Key for Chapter 16 Activity

**Easter Acrostic**

Possible words or phrases:

Eternal life

Angels' message (or teach the Greek word *anastasis*, meaning "resurrection," from which the name Anastasia is derived)

Saved us from death

Thomas doubted

Empty tomb

Risen Christ

Answer Keys

## Answer Key for Chapter 18 Activity

**W**isdom

**U**nderstanding

**R**ight Judgment

**C**ourage

**K**nowledge

**R**everence

**W**onder and Awe

Answer
Keys